STATUS OF WOMEN IN INDIA

STATUS OF WOMEN IN INDIA

DR. SHOBANA NELASCO
M.A., M.B.A., D.C.A., M.Phil., Ph.D.
Reader, Department of Economics
Fatima College, Madurai, T.N.

DEEP & DEEP PUBLICATIONS PVT. LTD.
F-159, Rajouri Garden, New Delhi - 110 027

STATUS OF WOMEN IN INDIA

ISBN 978-81-8450-246-6

Printed in India at MAYUR ENTERPRISES
WZ Plot No. 3, Gujjar Market, Tihar Village, New Delhi - 110 018

Published by DEEP & DEEP PUBLICATIONS PVT. LTD.,
F-159, Rajouri Garden, New Delhi - 110 027 • Phone : 25435369, 25440916
E-mail : ddpubs@gmail.com • ddpbooks@yahoo.co.in
Showroom :
2/13, Ansari Road, Daryaganj, New Delhi - 110 002 • Telefax : 23245122

You can tell the condition of a nation
by looking at the status of its women.

—Jawaharlal Nehru

Contents

Preface

The greatness of any civilization could be judged by the regard and respect shown by its men folk to the women of that society. The status of women in India has been subject to many great changes over the past. From a largely poorer status of women in ancient times, to the promotion of women rights by many reformers, the history of women in India has been eventful. Women in India started realizing that they are equal players in the family and nation building. One could say that they are even competitors for men, in every walk of life including politics and administration.

But still, the gender equality in all fields of life is continuing to be a debatable issue. Women are both revered as well as abused in the Indian society; sometimes even within her own home. Awareness about any problem becomes the starting point for solving the same. This book is an effort to explain the status of different categories of Indian women. Few of the excerpts are taken from the publications of the author's earlier works. The chapter on Domestic Violence Act may help the readers, especially the affected women, to protect themselves legally from the extreme form of chauvinistic male domination and harassment. Since it is a proven fact that the development of any country is directly proportional to the Gender Development Index, Indian Government should act more prudently to raise the status of women, the most important but vulnerable section of the society.

I thank my husband Mr. Nelasco for motivating me for writing more on women related issues. He has been instrumental in all my academic ventures. I also thank my sweet daughters Cherly and Junofy, who motivate and support me in all my academic endeavors. I realize the blessings of my late grandfather Mr. A.T. Dominic Paul Nadar who always prayed for my achievements. I also acknowledge the motivation given by all my friends, relatives and parents. I thank Rev. Mother Rose, Founder of Fatima College and all the sisters of St. Joseph of Lyons, whose main mission is empowerment of downtrodden women. I am also grateful to the publishers for their genuine interest towards the target of the book. Finally, I dedicate this book, all my academic contributions and all the honors that I have received to Lord Jesus Christ, for everything is purely the outcome of His Grace.

DR. SHOBANA NELASCO

1

Empowerment of Women in India

"Women themselves have the right to live in dignity, in freedom from want and freedom from fear. On this International Women's Day, let us rededicate ourselves to making that a reality".

—Kofi Annan

By development we mean the development of all sections of the society including both genders. A society cannot progress much, leaving women, out site the process of development activities. Earlier development theorists had assumed that the process of development trickle down from top to bottom and thus would automatically bring about an improvement of all sections across all gender. Unfortunately this did not work out well. Instead it resulted in the experience of social exclusion of one gender. Discrimination across gender is the most distressing fact cutting across caste, class and ethnic composition.

Like their male counterpart, women also play their important parts in the social, economic and cultural process directly or indirectly. Even in the traditional tribal societies women played the dominant role in the social and economic activity excepting the political process. In spite of this, they are long neglected in the sense of food and calorie intake, education, health care, political participation and also psychologically.

Traditionally, women are thought to be the symbol of sacrifice. They play simultaneous role of a daughter, sister, wife, mother and their activities were mainly confirmed within the boundary of four walls. Their main taste includes bearing and rearing of children, the household works and above all to satisfy all the members of the family. In many societies, especially in rural area, women take the responsibility of fetching drinking water, collecting fuel wood on well as take part in gardening and agricultural activities from sowing to harvest. Their role either as mother or wife in addition to other socio-economic performances has immense important in welfare of the society. Sometimes in the very poor families they themselves sustain without sufficient or nutritional in-take but try hard to fulfil the nutritional need of their male members in the family. Whereas in most cases because of the lack of recognition and due to the nature of works, non-marketing of their contribution, and proper evaluation of those activities by women have never been done. Their contribution to the society in however no less than their male counterpart. Even some researchers and famous sociologists thought women's role in traditional societies were more comprehensive, active, independent and valued.

Empowerment of women essentially brings a shift from unjust to just society. Empowerment of women refer to questioning the social, economic and political discrepancies and distortions. The term empowerment of women has come to be associated with women's struggle for social justice and equality.

Empowerment is all about power and about drawing the balance of power. It is the action of various factors namely physical, socio-economic, political, mental, psychological, attitudinal and so on. Women's empowerment could be described on a process in which women obtain control over resources. It is simply a method of empowering themselves for bringing a self-image and self-confidence.

Women constituting 50 percent of the population have long been neglected in their role as beneficiaries in the process of development. They are lagging behind *economically, socially, politically and economically* in the society. The women's position in employment, earning, education, health status and decision-making is not up to mark. In India, women in general, are relatively powerless with low work participation rate, little decision-making power and very little or no control over resources.

The following data speaks the true status of Indian women:

In 2001, Indian male literacy rate was 75.96% whereas the female literacy rate was just 54.28 per cent. In India, there is enough evidence to show that high female *literacy* rates are associated with low rates of population growth, infant mortality, maternal mortality and high rate of life expectancy. Further, it leads to better hygiene, improved nutritional practices, good family health and small family size thereby contributing to better living. But in India, female literacy rate is very low, when compared to male literacy in India.

The foremost important area is *economic empowerment*. Women's well-being is decided by the prospects for gainful *employment*. Women's employment not only creates self-confidence in them but also develops their bargaining power within the household. Further, the survival changes of female children increase as the employment of women rises and *earnings differentials between men and women* decreases. *Political empowerment* is also equally important for improving the well-being of the women. Thus, the overall development of women is imperative for the development of the society and the nation.

India, with a population of 989 million, is the world's second most populous country. Of that number, 120 million are women who live in poverty.

Over 70 percent of India's population currently derive their livelihood from land resources, which includes 84 percent of the economically-active women.

India is one of the few countries where males significantly outnumber females, and this imbalance has increased over time. India's maternal mortality rates in rural areas are among the world's highest. From a global perspective, Indian accounts for 19 percent of all lives births and 27 percent of all maternal deaths.

"There seems to be a consensus that higher female mortality between ages one and five and high maternal mortality rates result in a deficit of females in the population.

Chatterjee (1990) estimates that deaths of young girls in India exceed those of young boys by over 300,000 each year, and every sixth infant death is specifically due to gender discrimination." Of the 15 million baby girls born in India each year, nearly 25 percent will not live to see their 15th birthday.

"Although India was the first country to announce an official family planning program in 1952, its population grew from 361 million in 1951 to 844 million in 1991. India's total fertility rate of 3.8 births per woman is considered moderate by world standards."

Since 1970, the use of modern contraceptive methods has risen from 10 percent to 40 percent, with great variance between northern and southern India. The most striking aspect of contraceptive use in India is the predominance of sterilization, which accounts for more than 85 percent of total modern contraception use, with female sterilization accounting for 90 percent of all sterilizations.

The origin of the Indian idea of appropriate female behavior can be traced to the rules laid down by Manu in 200 B.C.: "by a young girl, by a young woman, or even by an aged one, nothing must be done independently, even in her own house". "In childhood a female must be subject to her father, in youth to her husband, when her lord is dead to her sons; a woman must never be independent."

A report commissioned by the United Nations Resident Co-ordinator in India (Menon-Sen and Shivakumar, 2001) titled 'Women in India: How Free? How Equal?'

raises several disturbing issues concerning the current status of women in India. The study's main findings are outlined below. Data from the Census of India 2001 and the Human Development Report 2001 also corroborate some of the study's observations.

These include: Although the absolute number of females has grown 21.79 percent in the last decade, the male-female ratio is still lower than it was 100 years ago. In societies where men and women are treated equally, women tend to outlive and outnumber men.

Typically, one would expect to find 103-105 women for every 100 men. The 2001 Census reveals an adverse ratio of 93 women for every 100 men. With the exception of Kerala, every state has fewer women than men. India, in the words of Amartya Sen, has to account for some 25 million 'missing women'. The Indian girl child is disadvantaged right from birth. The sex ratio for girl children between the age of 0 and 6 years is 927, strengthening the fear that some girl children are never born or have no opportunity to survive.

- Only 54 percent of women are literate as compared to 76 percent of men.
- More than 36 percent of the population lives below the poverty line. Many of them are women.
- There are far fewer women in the paid workforce than are men.
- In some states such as West Bengal, Orissa, Bihar, Assam and Arunachal Pradesh, between 63 and 85 percent of married women suffer from anaemia (IIPS, 2000 and ORC Macro, 2000).
- The average Indian woman bears her first child before she is 22 years and has little control over her own fertility and reproductive health. In 1998-99, only 48 percent of married women in the reproductive age group used Police records for the country as a whole show that a woman is molested every 26 minutes. A rape occurs every 34 minutes. Every 42 minutes, an incident of sexual harassment takes place. A woman is kidnapped every 43 minutes. And every 93 minutes, a woman is killed. Any form of contraception (World Population Monitoring, 2000). This figure is much lower (30%) in poorer states like Uttar Pradesh and Bihar.
- For many women, abortion is the only method of contraception available.
- More than 570 women die per 100,000 births (World Population Monitoring, 2000), 70 percent due to totally avoidable reasons.
- Women are under-represented in governance and decision-making positions.
- Most women do not have any autonomy in decision-making in their personal lives.
- In Madhya Pradesh and Rajasthan, less than 50 percent

of women have access to money in the household (IIPS and ORC Macro, 2000).

- Women face violence inside and outside their family, as well as at the workplace.

The impact of drug use on women, both directly and indirectly, needs to be understood within the context of these realities.

> *"there is no tool for development more effective than the empowerment of women."*
>
> —Kofi Annan

> *'When women thrive, all of society benefits, and succeeding generations are given a better start in life'.*
>
> —Kofi Annan

2

Historical Status of Women in India

The status of women in India has been subject to many great changes over the past few millennia. From a largely unknown status in ancient times through the low points of the medieval period, to the promotion of equal rights by many reformers, the history of women in India has been eventful.

WOMEN STATUS IN ANCIENT INDIA

Some scholars believe that in ancient India, the women enjoyed equal status with men in all fields of life. However, some others hold contrasting views. Works by ancient Indian grammarians such as Patanjali and Katyayana suggest that women were educated in the early Vedic period. Rigvedic verses suggest that the women married at a mature age and were probably free to select their husband. Scriptures such as Rig Veda and Upanishads mention several women sages and seers, notably Gargi and Maitreyi.

Some kingdoms in the ancient India had traditions such as *nagarvadhu* ("bride of the city"). Women competed to win the coveted title of the *nagarvadhu*. Amrapali is the most famous example of a *nagarvadhu*.

According to studies, women enjoyed equal status and rights during the early Vedic period. However, later (approximately 500 B.C.), the status of women began to decline with the Smritis (esp. Manusmriti) and with the Islamic invasion of Babur and the Mughal empire and later Christianity curtailing women's freedom and rights.

Although reformatory movements such as Jainism allowed women to be admitted to the religious order, by and large, the women in India faced confinement and restrictions. The practice of child marriage is believed to have started from around sixth century.

WOMEN STATUS IN MEDIEVAL PERIOD

Indian woman's position in the society further deteriorated during the medieval period. Sati, child marriages and ban on widow remarriages became part of social life in India. The Muslim conquest in the Indian subcontinent brought the purdah practice in the Indian society. Among the Rajputs of Rajasthan, the Jauhar was practised. In some parts of India, the Devadasis or the temple women were sexually exploited. Polygamy was widely practised esp. among Hindu Kshatriya rulers. In many Muslim families, women were secluded to Zenana.

In spite of these conditions, some women execeled in the fields of politics, literature, education and religion. Razia Sultana became the only woman monarch to have ever ruled Delhi. The Gond queen Durgavati ruled for fifteen years, before she lost her life in a battle with Mughal emperor Akbar's general Asaf Khan in 1564. Chand Bibi defended Ahmednagar against the mighty Mughal forces of Akbar in 1590s. Jehangir's wife Nur Jehan effectively wielded imperial power and was recognized as the real force behind the Mughal throne. Shivaji's mother, Jijabai was deputed as queen regent, because of her ability as a warrior and administrator. In South India, many women administered villages, towns, divisions and heralded social and religious institutions.

The Bhakti cults tried to restore women's status and questioned some of the forms of oppression. Mirabai, a female saint-poet, was one of the most important Bhakti movement figures. Some other female saint-poets from this period include Akkamadevi, Rani Janabai and Lal Ded.

Bhakti sects within Hinduism such as the Mahanubhav, Varkari and many others were principle movements within the Hindu fold to openly advocate social justice and equality between men and women.

Jahanara Begum and Princess Zebunnissa were well-known poetesses and they also influenced the ruling administration.

Shortly after the Bhakti movement, Guru Nanak, the first Guru of Sikhs also preached the message of equality between men and women. He advocated that women be allowed to lead religious assemblies; to perform and lead congregational hymn singing called Kirtan or Bhajan; become members of religious management committees; to lead armies on the battlefield; have equality in marriage, and equality in Amrit (Baptism). Other Sikh Gurus also preached against the discrimination against women.

HISTORICAL PRACTICES

Traditions such as sati, jauhar, child marriage, and devadasi have been banned and are largely defunct. However, some cases of these practices are still found in remote parts of India. The purdah is still practised by many Indian women.

Sati

Sati is an old, largely defunct custom, in which the widow was immolated alive on her husband's funeral pyre. Although the act was supposed to be a voluntary on the widow's part, it is believed to have been sometimes forced on the widow. It was abolished by the British in 1829. There have been around forty reported cases of sati since independence. In 1987, the Roop Kanwar case of Rajasthan led to The Commission of Sati (Prevention) Act.

Jauhar

Jauhar refers to the practice of the voluntary immolation of all the wives and daughters of defeated warriors, in order to avoid capture and consequent molestation by the enemy. The practice was followed by the wives of defeated Rajput rulers, who are known to place a high premium on honour.

Child Marriages

Earlier, child marriages were highly prevalent in India. The young girls would live with their parents till they reached puberty. In the past, the child widows were condemned to a life of great agony, shaving heads, living in isolation, and shunned by the society. Although child marriage was outlawed in 1860, it is still a common practice in some underdeveloped areas of the country.

Purdah

Purdah is the practice of requiring women to cover their bodies so as to cover their skin and conceal their form. It imposes restrictions on the mobility of women, it curtails their right to interact freely and it is a symbol of the subordination of women. It does not reflect the religious teachings of either Hinduism or Islam, contrary to common belief, although misconception has occurred due to the ignorance and prejudices of religious leaders of both faiths.

Devadasis

Devadasi is a religious practice in some parts of southern India, in which women are "married" to a deity or temple. The ritual was well established by the 10th century A.D. In the later period, the illegitimate sexual exploitation of the devadasis became a norm in some parts of India.

WOMEN STATUS DURING BRITISH PERIOD

European scholars observed in the 19th century Hindu women are "naturally chaste" and "more virtuous" than other women. During the British Raj, many reformers such as Ram Mohan Roy, Ishwar Chandra Vidyasagar, Jyotirao Phule, etc. fought for the upliftment of women. Raja Rammohun Roy's efforts led to the abolition of the Sati practice in 1829. Ishwar Chandra Vidyasagar's crusade for the improvement in condition of widows led to the Widow Remarriage Act of 1856. Many women reformers such as Pandita Ramabai also helped the cause of women upliftment.

Rani Lakshmi Bai, the Queen of Jhansi, led the Indian Rebellion of 1857 against the British. She is now widely considered as a nationalist hero. Begum Hazrat Mahal, the co-ruler of Awadh, was another ruler who led the revolt of 1857. She refused the deals with the British and later retreated to Nepal. The Begums of Bhopal were also few of the notable female rulers during this period. They did not observe purdah and were trained in martial arts.

Chandramukhi Basu, Kadambini Ganguly and Anandi Gopal Joshi were few of the earliest Indian women to obtain educational degrees.

In 1917, the first women's delegation met the Secretary of State to demand women's political rights, supported by the Indian National Congress. The All India Women's Education Conference was held in Pune in 1927. In 1929, the Child Marriage Restraint Act was passed, stipulating fourteen as the minimum age of marriage for a girl through the efforts of Mahomed Ali Jinnah. Though Mahatma Gandhi himself married at the age of thirteen, he later urged people to boycott child marriages and called upon the young men to marry the child widows.

Women played an important part in India's independence struggle. Some of the famous freedom fighters include Bhikaji Cama, Dr. Annie Besant, Pritilata Waddedar, Vijayalakshmi Pandit, Rajkumari Amrit Kaur, Anjali Ammal, Aruna Asaf Ali, Sucheta Kriplani and Kasturba Gandhi. Other notable names include Muthulakshmi Reddy, Durgabai Deshmukh, etc. The Rani of Jhansi Regiment of Subhash Chandra Bose's Indian National Army consisted entirely of women including Captain Lakshmi Sahgal. Sarojini Naidu, a poet and a freedom fighter, was the first Indian woman to become the President of the Indian National Congress and the first woman to become the governor of a state in India.

WOMEN STATUS IN INDEPENDENT INDIA

Women in India now participate in all activities such as education, politics, media, art and culture, service sectors, science and technology, etc. The Constitution of India guarantees to all Indian women equality (Article 14), no discrimination by the State (Article 15(1)), equality of opportunity (Article 16), equal pay for equal work (Article 39(d)). In addition, it allows special provisions to be made by the State in favour of women and children (Article 15(3)), renounces practices derogatory to the dignity of women (Article 51(A) (e)), and also allows for provisions to be made by the State for securing just and humane conditions of work and for maternity relief. (Article 42).

The feminist activism in India picked up momentum during later 1970s. One of the first national level issues that brought the women's groups together was the Mathura rape case. The acquittal of policemen accused of raping a young girl Mathura in a police station, led to a wide-scale protests in 1979-80. The protests were widely covered in the national media, and forced the Government to amend the Evidence Act, the Criminal Procedure Code and the Indian Penal Code and introduce the category of custodial rape. Female activists united over issues such as female infanticide, gender bias, women health, and female literacy.

Since alcoholism is often associated with violence against women in India, many women groups launched anti-liquor campaigns. Many Indian Muslim women have questioned the fundamental leaders' interpretation of women's rights under the Shariat law and have criticized the triple talaq system.

In 1990s, grants from foreign donor agencies enabled the formation of new women-oriented NGOs. Self-help groups and NGOs such as Self Employed Women's Association (SEWA) have played a major role in women's rights in India. Many women have emerged as leaders of local movements. For example, Medha Patkar of the Narmada Bachao Andolan.

The Government of India declared 2001 as the Year of Women's Empowerment (*Swashakti*). The National Policy For The Empowerment of Women was passed in 2001.

Contrary to the common perception, a large percent of women in India work. The National data collection agencies accept the fact that there is a serious under-estimation of women's contribution as workers. However, there are far fewer women in the paid workforce than there are men. In urban India, Women have impressive number in the workforce. As an example at software industry 30% of the workforce is female.

They are at par with their male counter parts in terms of wages, position at the work place.

In rural India, agriculture and allied industrial sectors employ as much as 89.5% of the total female labour. In overall farm production, women's average contribution is estimated at 55% to 66% of the total labour. According to a 1991 World Bank report, women accounted for 93% of total employment in dairy production in India. Women constitute 51% of the total employed in forest-based small-scale enterprises.

One of the most famous female business success stories is the Shri Mahila Griha Udyog, the makers of the Lijjat papad. In 2006, Kiran Mazumdar-Shaw, who started Biocon—one of India's first biotech companies, was rated India's richest woman. Lalita Gupte and Kalpana Morparia (both were the only businesswomen in India who made our list of the Forbes World's Most Powerful Women), run India's second-largest bank, ICICI Bank.

CHANGE IN STATUS OF WOMEN IN INDIA

By the dawn of 20th century women become more aware of their social position and started utilising their potential. Hence there is a substantial rise in their development. In some fields they even supersede men. The steady change in their position can be highlighted by looking at what has been achieved by women in the country:

- 1905: Suzanne R.D. Tata becomes the first Indian woman to drive a car.
- 1916: The first women's university, SNDT Women's University, was founded on June 2, 1916 by the social reformer Dhondo Keshav Karve with just five students.
- 1927: The All India Women's Conference was founded.
- 1994: Harita Kaur Deol becomes the first Indian woman to perform a solo flight.
- 1951: Prem Mathur becomes the first Indian woman commercial pilot of the Deccan Airways
- 1959: Anna Chandy becomes the first Indian woman Judge of High Court.

- 1966: Captain Durga Banerjee becomes the first Indian woman pilot of the state airline, Indian Airlines.
- 1966: Kamaladevi Chattopadhyay wins Ramon Magsaysay award for community leadership.
- 1966: Indira Gandhi becomes the first woman Prime Minister of India
- 1970: Kamaljit Sandhu becomes the first Indian woman to win a Gold in the Asian Games
- 1972: Kiran Bedi becomes the first female recruit to join the Indian Police Service.
- 1989: Justice M. Fathima Beevi becomes the first woman judge of the Supreme Court of India.
- November 1997: Kalpana Chawla becomes the first Indian woman to go into Space.
- September 21, 1992: Priya Jhingan becomes the first lady cadet to join the Indian Army (later commissioned on March 6, 1993).
- 2004: Punita Arora becomes the first woman in the Indian Army to don the highest rank of Lt General.
- 2005: Manndhir Rajput, a 34-year-old woman from Ludhiana, Punjab, becomes the first Indian woman to become an engine driver of trains with the New South Wales Rail Corporation, Australia.
- 2007: Pratibha Patil becomes the first woman President of India.

3

Discrimination and Evils against Women in India

However much a mother may love her children, it is all but impossible for her to provide high-quality child care if she herself is poor and oppressed, illiterate and uninformed, anaemic and unhealthy, has five or six other children, lives in a slum or shanty, has neither clean water nor safe sanitation, and if she is without the necessary support either from health services, or from her society, or from the father of her children.

—Vulimiri Ramalingaswami, "The Asian Enigma"

Exploitation of women, oppression of women, male chauvinism, male ego, male dominance and patriarchy are some of the synonymous words used as themes for debates, workshops and researches. These are the concepts which are associated with the slow growth of women and their contribution towards their society. The better half part of our society, which constitutes nearly 50 per cent of the population, could not get its equal share, because it forms the group called women. Empowerment of women is the basic necessity to tap the 50 per cent potential of our human resource.

SEVEN MAJOR AREAS OF DISCRIMINATION AGAINST WOMEN IN INDIA

Carol S. Coonrod (1998), specifies seven major areas of discrimination against women in India. They are:

- *Malnutrition:* India has exceptionally high rates of child malnutrition, because tradition in India requires that women eat last and least throughout their lives, even when pregnant and lactating. Malnourished women give birth to malnourished children, perpetuating the cycle.
- *Poor Health:* Females receive less health care than males. Many women die in childbirth of easily prevented complications. Working conditions and environmental pollution further impairs women's health.
- *Lack of education*: Families are far less likely to educate girls than boys, and far more likely to pull them out of school, either to help out at home or from fear of violence.
- *Overwork*: Women work longer hours and their work is more arduous than men's, yet their work is unrecognized. Men report that "women, like children, eat and do nothing." Technological progress in agriculture has had a negative impact on women.
- *Unskilled*: In women's primary employment sector-agriculture—extension services overlook women.
- *Mistreatment:* In recent years, there has been an alarming rise in atrocities against women in India, in terms of rapes, assaults and dowry-related murders. Fear of violence suppresses the aspirations of all women. Female infanticide and sex-selective abortions are additional forms of violence that reflect the devaluing of females in Indian society.
- *Powerlessness*: While women are guaranteed equality under the constitution, legal protection has little effect in the face of prevailing patriarchal traditions. Women lack power to decide who they will marry, and are

often married off as children. Legal loopholes are used to deny women inheritance rights.

Most of the areas of discriminations are discussed elaborately discussed in this book. But the few left out areas like health, family planning and work force participation are explained below.

HEALTH

The average female life expectancy today in India is low compared to many countries, but it has shown gradual improvement over the years. In many families, esp. rural ones, the girls and women face nutritional discrimination within the family, and are anaemic and malnourished..

The maternal mortality in India is the second highest in the world. Only 42% of births in the country are supervised by health professionals. Most women deliver with help from women in the family who often lack the skills and resources to save the mother's life if it is in danger. According to UNDP Human Development Report (1997), the proportion of pregnant women (age 15-49) with anemia was found to be as high as 88%.

FAMILY PLANNING

The average Indian woman has little control over her own fertility and reproductive health. Women, particularly women in rural areas, do not have access to safe and self-controlled methods of contraception. The public health system emphasises permanent methods like sterilisation, or long-term methods like IUDs that do not need follow-up. Sterilization accounts for more than 75% of total contraception, with female sterilisation accounting for almost 95% of all sterilisations

LAND AND PROPERTY RIGHTS

In most Indian families, women do not own any property in their own names, and do not get a share of parental property. Due to weak enforcement of laws protecting them, women continue to have little access to land and property. In fact, some of the laws discriminate against women, when it comes to land and property rights.

The Hindu personal laws of mid-1956s (applied to Hindus, Buddhists, Sikhs and Jains) gave women rights to inheritance. However, the sons had an independent share in the ancestral property, while the daughters' shares were based on the share received by their father. Hence, a father could effectively disinherit a daughter by renouncing his share of the ancestral property, but the son will continue to have a share in his own right. Additionally, married daughters, even those facing marital harassment, had no residential rights in the ancestral home. After amendment of Hindu laws in 2005, now women have been provided the same status as that of men.

In 1986, the Supreme Court of India ruled that Shah Bano, an old divorced Muslim woman was eligible for maintenance money. However, the decision was vociferously opposed by fundamentalist Muslim leaders, who alleged that the court was interfering in their personal law. The Union Government subsequently passed the Muslim Women's (Protection of Rights Upon Divorce) Act.

Similarly, the Christian women have struggled over years for equal rights of divorce and succession. In 1994, all the churches, jointly with women's organisations, drew up a draft law called the Christian Marriage and Matrimonial Causes Bill. However, the government has still not amended the relevant laws.

CRIMES AGAINST WOMEN

Police records show high incidence of crimes against women in India. The National Crime Records Bureau reported in 1998 that the growth rate of crimes against women would be higher than the population growth rate by 2010. Earlier, many cases were not registered with the police due to the social stigma attached to rape and molestation cases. Official statistics show that there has been a dramatic increase in the number of reported crimes against women.

SEXUAL HARASSMENT

Half of the total number of crimes against women reported in 1990 related to molestation and harassment at the workplace. Eve teasing is a euphemism used for sexual harassment or molestation of women by men. Many activists blame the rising incidents of sexual harassment against women on the influence of "Western culture". In 1987, The Indecent Representation of Women (Prohibition) Act was passed to prohibit indecent representation of women through advertisements or in publications, writings, paintings, figures or in any other manner.

In 1997, in a landmark judgement, the Supreme Court of India took a strong stand against sexual harassment of women in the workplace. The Court also laid down detailed guidelines for prevention and redressal of grievances. The National Commission for Women subsequently elaborated these guidelines into a Code of Conduct for employers.

DOWRY

In 1961, the Government of India passed the Dowry Prohibition Act, making the dowry demands in wedding arrangements illegal. However, many cases of dowry-related domestic violence, suicides and murders have been reported. In the 1980s, numerous such cases were reported.

In 1985, the Dowry Prohibition (maintenance of lists of presents to the bride and bridegroom) rules were framed. According to these rules, a signed list of presents given at the time of the marriage to the bride and the bridegroom should be maintained. The list should contain a brief description of each present, its approximate value, the name of whoever has given the present and his/her relationship to the person. However, such rules are hardly enforced.

A 1997 report claimed that at least 5,000 women die each year because of dowry deaths, and at least a dozen die each day in 'kitchen fires' thought to be intentional. The term for this is "bride burning" and is criticized within India itself. Amongst the urban educated, such dowry abuse has reduced dramatically.

FEMALE INFANTICIDES AND SEX SELECTIVE ABORTIONS

India has a low sex ratio, the chief reason being that many women die before reaching adulthood. Tribal societies in India have a better sex ratio than all other caste groups. This, in spite of the fact that tribal communities have far lower levels of income, literacy and health facilities. It is therefore suggested by many experts, that the low sex ratio in India can be attributed to female infanticides and sex-selective abortions.

All medical tests that can be used to determine the sex of the child have been banned in India, due to incidents of these tests being used to get rid of unwanted female children before birth. Female infanticide (killing of girl infants) is still prevalent in some rural areas. The abuse of the dowry tradition has been one of the main reasons for sex-selective abortions and female infanticides in India.

DOMESTIC VIOLENCE

The incidents of domestive violence are higher among the lower Socio-Economic Classes (SECs). There are various instances of an inebriated husband beating up the wife often leading to severe injuries. Domestic violence is also seen in the form of physical abuse. The Protection of Women from Domestic Violence Act, 2005 came into force on October 26, 2006.

TRAFFICKING

The Immoral Traffic (Prevention) Act was passed in 1956. However, many cases of trafficking of young girls and women have been reported. These women are either forced into prostitution, domestic work or child labor.

INHERITANCE

Women's rights to inheritance are limited and frequently violated. In the mid-1950s the Hindu personal laws, which apply to all Hindus, Buddhists, Sikhs and Jains, were overhauled, banning polygamy and giving women rights to inheritance, adoption and divorce. The Muslim personal laws differ considerably from that of the Hindus, and permit polygamy. Despite various laws protecting women's rights, traditional patriarchal attitudes still prevail and are strengthened and perpetuated in the home.

Under Hindu law, sons have an independent share in the ancestral property. However, daughters' shares are based on the share received by their father. Hence, a father can effectively disinherit a daughter by renouncing his share of the ancestral property, but the son will continue to have a share in his own right. Additionally, married daughters, even those facing marital harassment, have no residential rights in the ancestral home.

Even the weak laws protecting women have not been adequately enforced. As a result, in practice, women continue to have little access to land and property, a major source of income and long-term economic security. Under the pretext of preventing fragmentation of agricultural holdings, several states have successfully excluded widows and daughters from inheriting agricultural land.

4

Inter-State Position of Women in India

The women empowerment among states shows a wide disparity in India. Inter-state variation with respect to various indicators of development may be highlighted with the help of relativity. Kerala is the only state, which is performing well in almost all the indicators of social development. The state of Kerala with a literacy rate of 87.86% is the highest among the states, the lowest female infant mortality rate and high mean age at effective marriage (i.e.) 22 yrs. In fact, Kerala's birth, death, infant mortality and literacy rates compare favourably even with some of the developed countries.

Punjab state has failed to improve the female position in Punjab. There seems to be an inverse relationship between the per capita income and sex ratio, which indicates that discrimination against women and female child continues unabatedly.

Maharashtra is behind Kerala, in mean age at effective marriage. But in case of crude birth rate and crude death rate, they overtake Kerala. In Maharashtra the distinction having

TABLE 4.1
Inter-State Position of Women

State	Female literacy	Female sex ratio	Female work participation	Female enrolment at university	Percentage of women with anaemia	Female dropout rate	Crime rate against women
(1)	(2)	(3)	(4)	(5)	(6)	(7)	(8)
Andhra Pradesh	51.17	978	40.2	31.8	49.8	41.23	143
Arunachal Pradesh	44.24	901	45.0	22.9	62.7	50.81	123
Assam	56.03	932	24.9	33.5	69.7	42.20	130
Bihar	33.57	921	23.5	18.9	63.4	58.64	54
Chhattisgarh	52.40	990	48.0				
Chandigarh				51.5		-66.17	
Delhi		821		45.3	40.5	6.03	
Goa	75.51	960	24.8		36.4	11.51	61
Gujarat	58.60	921	30.9	40.1	46.3	28.10	139
Haryana	56.31	861	32.1	39.3	47.0	12.78	152
Jammu and Kashmir	41.82	900	25.7	40.6	58.7	47.39	184
Karnataka	57.45	964	36.6	34.6	42.4	27.19	74
Kerala	87.86	1058	17.2	53.6	22.7	-5	153
Madhya Pradesh	50.28	920		30.5	54.3	22.97	206

(*Contd.*)

TABLE 4.1 (Contd.)

(1)	(2)	(3)	(4)	(5)	(6)	(7)	(8)
Maharashtra	67.51	922	40.1	37.0	48.7	21.72	151
Manipur	59.70	978	46.2	43.4	28.9	42.90	39
Meghalaya	60.41	975	43.7	40.1	63.3	57.22	33
Sikkim	61.46	875	45.5	36.3	61.1	56.35	75
Mizoram	86.13	938	56.8	40.1	48	51.27	171
Nagaland	61.92	909	44.8	40.1	38.4	46.68	18
Orissa	50.92	972	28.6	32.7	63.0	44.38	121
Punjab	63.55	874	21.2	51.5	41.1	20.15	53
Rajasthan	44.34	922	41.0	33.0	48.5	62.68	231
Tamil Nadu	64.55	986	35.1	40.1	56.5	39.19	83
West Bengal	60.22	934	21.0	36.3	62.7	58.48	8.9
Uttar Pradesh	42.98	898	20.0	27.0		62.16	103
Uttaranchal	60.26		31.9				

Sources: 1. Preeti Rastogi, 'Significance of gender related development indicators', Indian Journal of Gender Studies, Volume II, No. 3, Sept.-Dec. 2004.

2. Mariama, A. Varghese, 'Women's Education, Educational Policies in India' K. Sudha Rao (Ed.), NIEPA, New Delhi.

highest female wade participation. The state also has a lowest maternal mortality ratio.

MALE-FEMALE LITERACY GAP IN VARIOUS STATES OF INDIA

It is miserable to see in all the states the female literacy is low when compared to male literacy. This female-male literacy gap is the lowest in Mizoram in 1991 (7.01) and in 2001 (4.56). The table shows few states like Mizoram, Megalaya and Kerala are having less literacy gap, whereas Rajasthan, Uttaranchal, Uttar Pradesh and Jharkhand are the states having excess of Male-Female literacy gap in 1991.

TABLE 4.2
Inter-state Male-Female Literacy Gap

Year / *States*	*1991*			*2001*		
	Male Literacy	*Female Literacy*	*Gap in Literacy*	*Male Literacy*	*Female Literacy*	*Gap in Literacy*
(1)	*(2)*	*(3)*	*(4)*	*(5)*	*(6)*	*(7)*
India	64.13	39.28	24.85	75.96	54.28	21.68
Andhra Pradesh	55.13	32.72	22.42	70.85	51.17	19.68
Arunachal Pradesh	51.45	29.69	21.76	64.07	44.34	19.83
Assam	61.89	43.03	18.84	71.93	56.03	15.90
Bihar	51.37	21.99	29.38	60.32	33.57	26.75
Chhattisgarh	58.07	27.52	30.54	77.86	52.4	25.46
Goa	83.64	67.09	16.55	88.88	75.51	13.37
Gujarat	73.39	48.92	24.47	80.5	58.6	21.90
Haryana	69.1	40.47	28.62	79.26	56.31	22.94
Himachal Pradesh	75.41	52.26	23.16	86.02	68.08	17.94
Jammu & Kashmir				75.96	54.28	23.93
Jharkhand	55.8	25.52	30.28	67.94	39.38	28.57
Karnataka	67.26	44.34	22.93	76.29	57.45	18.84
Kerala	93.62	86.17	7.45	94.2	87.86	6.34
Madhya Pradesh	58.54	29.35	29.19	76.80	50.28	26.52
Maharashtra	76.56	52.32	24.24	86.27	67.51	18.75

(Contd

TABLE 4.2 (*Contd.*)

(1)	(2)	(3)	(4)	(5)	(6)	(7)
Manipur*	71.63	47.6	24.03	77.87	59.7	18.17
Meghalaya	53.12	44.85	8.27	66.14	60.41	5.73
Mizoram	85.61	78.6	7.01	90.69	86.13	4.5
Nagaland	67.62	54.75	12.87	71.77	61.92	9.85
Orissa	63.09	34.68	28.41	75.95	50.97	24.98
Punjab	65.66	50.41	15.26	75.63	63.55	12.08
Rajasthan	54.99	20.44	34.55	76.46	44.34	32.12
Sikkim	65.7	46.76	18.94	76.73	61.46	15.2
Tamil Nadu	73.75	51.33	22.42	82.33	64.55	17.78
Tripura	70.58	49.65	20.93	81.47	65.41	15.06
Uttar Pradesh	54.82	24.37	30.46	70.23	42.98	27.25
Uttaranchal	72.79	41.63	31.17	84.01	60.26	23.75
West Bengal	67.81	46.56	21.25	77.56	60.22	17.35

Source : Census of India Report.

This gender literacy gap is a major stumbling block for the development of any country. It means that one gender is favoured for education. Another major issue of this analysis is that between 1991 and 2001 the literacy rate of male and female gender is improving but the disparity continues. The differences in literacy rates among the states are also extreme. Kerala has the highest female literacy rate both in 1990-91 and 2000-01. The state with the second highest female literacy is Mizoram. And Goa is standing third in the row. On the other hand, the order of women literacy is reshuffled in the year 2000-01. Rajastan is ranked first, Bihar, the second, U.P., Jharkhand are the successors in 1990-91. Wheras in 2000-01, the order is Bihar, Jharkhand, U.P. and Rajasthan. In other words, while Rajasthan was topping the list of female literacy in 1990-91, in 2000-01 Bihar is pushed back to top the list.

Looking at the gender gulf, in 1990-91 the Rajastan, Uttaranchal, U.P. and Jharkhand are having the wider gender literacy gap; in 2000-01 the order is changed as Rajasthan, Jharkhand, U.P. and Bihar. In both the periods the gender literacy gap is very high in Rajasthan.

As with India as a whole, many states have large rural-urban differences in female literacy. In 6 of the 24 states, 25 percent or less of the women in rural areas are literate. In Rajasthan, less than 12 percent of rural women are literate. In 1992-93, 75 percent of boys and 61 percent of girls aged 6 to 10 years were attending school. There are large differences in school attendance by state. In six states, over 85 percent of girls aged 6 to 14 were attending school. Not surprisingly, these states also had female literacy rates that were above the national average. In all states except Bihar, Rajasthan, and Uttar Pradesh, more than half of the girls aged 6 to 14 were attending school.

5

Status of Indian Women in the World

The first literature appeared some 4,000 years ago. Stone and bone records stretch back further than those first alphabets, but give us no names. The very first technical name was male—Imhotep—the architect of the first pyramid. The second technical name was female En Hedu'Anna (c. 2354 BC). Women have been physicians in great numbers ever since there have been women. Midwifery was almost exclusively run by women until the 19th century.

But invariably in all fields both in developed and developing countries women potential is not tapped fully. Since 1901, there have been over three hundred recipients of the Nobel Prize in the Sciences; only ten of them (3 per cent) are women.

Considering Indian environment, constitutionally and legally women enjoy the unique status of equality with men. In spite of all efforts, the female population ratio, the female literacy ratio, female employment ratio, female school or college enrolment ratio, etc., continue to be at a lower rate. Our cultural history and Political history has proved that women were considered as a secondary human being. The birth of a son is bliss incarnate, while that of a daughter is the root of family misery. Only the sons are the heirs of their parents and they are eligible to do the final rites of their parents. Almost all the religions project women inferior to men.

In India, for instance, according to the 1981 census, there are as many as 935 women for every 1000 men—the women's share in employment is only 21 per cent. The Indian average female-male ratio (FMR) of 0.93 (2001 census) is the second lowest in the world (after Pakistan) lower than the FMR of sub-Saharan Africa. The percentage of female labour force compared to the total labour force is just 28.5 per cent in 1991.

Amartya Sen points out that when he took up issues of women's welfare, he was accused in India of voicing "foreign concerns." "I was told Indian women don't think like that about equality. But I would like to argue that if they don't think like that they should be given a real opportunity to think like that." Parmita Shastri, *Outlook India*, 1998.

In India, for instance, according to the 1981 census, there are as many as 935 women for every 1000 men—the women's share in employment is only 21 per cent. Indian position in the global index is very low in most of the economic, social and political indicators. India stood in 128th position in the World Human Development Index.

A COMPARATIVE ANALYSIS OF INDIAN H.D.I IN THE WORLD

Each year, since 1990 the Human Development Report has published the Human Development Index (HDI). This gives a broader definition of well-being. The HDI provides a composite measure of three dimensions of human development: living a long and healthy life (measured by life expectancy), being educated (measured by adult literacy and enrolment at the primary, secondary and tertiary level) and having a decent standard of living (measured by purchasing power parity, PPP, income). The index is not in any sense a comprehensive measure of human development. The following table shows that India with its HDI value of 0.619, stands much backward rank of 128th out of 177 countries.

TABLE 5.1

Position of Indian HDI in the World 2005

HDI Value	*Life expectancy at birth (years)*	*Adult literacy rate (% ages 15 and older)*	*Combined primary, secondary and tertiary gross enrolment ratio (%)*	*GDP per capita (PPP US $)*
(1)	*(2)*	*(3)*	*(4)*	*(5)*
1. Iceland (0.968)	1. Japan (82.3)	1. Georgia (100.0)	1. Australia (113.0)	1. Luxembourg (60,228)
126. Morocco (0.646)	123. Pakistan (64.6)	112. Rwanda (64.9)	120. Namibia (64.7)	115. Syrian Arab Republic (3,808)
127. Equatorial Guinea (0.642)	124. Comoros (64.1)	113. Malawi (64.1)	121. Viet Nam (63.9)	116. Nicaragua (3,674)
128. India (0.619)	125. India (63.7)	114. India (61.0)	122. India (63.8)	117. India (3,452)
129. Solomon Islands (0.602)	126. Mauritania (63.2)	115. Sudan (60.9)	123. Vanuatu (63.4)	118. Honduras (3,430)
130. Lao People's Democratic Republic (0.601)	127. Lao People's Democratic Republic (63.2)	116. Burundi (59.3)	124. Malawi (63.1)	119. Georgia (3,365)
177. Sierra Leone (0.336)	177. Zambia (40.5)	139. Burkina Faso (23.6)	172. Niger (22.7)	174. Malawi (667)

Source : Human Development Index, UNDP.

But this HDI does not include important indicators such as poverty, unemployment, income inequality, respect for human rights, political freedoms and the foremost of all the gender inequality.

THE GDI COMPARED TO THE HDI

The HDI measures average achievements in a country, but it does not incorporate the degree of gender imbalance in these achievements. The gender-related development index (GDI), introduced in Human Development Report, 1995, measures achievements in the same dimensions using the same indicators as the HDI but captures inequalities in achievement between women and men. It is simply the HDI adjusted downward for gender inequality. The greater the gender disparity in basic human development, the lower is a country's GDI relative to its HDI. India's GDI value, 0.600 should be compared to its HDI value of 0.619. Its GDI value is 96.9% of its HDI value. Out of the 156 countries with both HDI and GDI values, 137 countries have a better ratio than India's.

Table 5.2 shows how India's ratio of GDI to HDI compares to other countries, and also shows its values for selected underlying values in the calculation of the GDI.

GENDER DEVELOPMENT INDEX (GDI) FOR INDIA

India stands in 112th position in *Gender-related development index* in 2005 with a value of 0.6. This Gender Related Index is calculated by Female (65.3) and Male (62.3) Life Expectancy at birth, Male (73.4) and Female (47.8) Adult Literacy Rate, Male (68%) and Female (60%) Combined Gross Enrolment Ratio for primary, secondary and tertiary Education, Estimated Male (5,194 PPP US$) and Female (1,620 PPP US$) estimated earned income and HDI rank minus GDI rank.

GENDER EMPOWERMENT MEASURE (GEM) FOR INDIA

India is ranked 95th (0.228) in the World-Gender Empowerment measure (GEM) in 1995. *Gender Empowerment Measure* is calculated by the percentage of women seats (9%) in

TABLE 5.2
Indian Position of GDI Compared to the HDI

GDI as % of HDI	*Life expectancy at birth (years) 2004 (Female as % male)*	*Adult literacy rate (% ages 15 and older) 2004 (Female as % male)*	*Combined primary, secondary and Certiary gross enrolment ratio 2004 (Female as % male)*
(1)	*(2)*	*(3)*	*(4)*
1. Maldives (100.4%)	1. Russian Federation (123.1%)	1. Lesotho (122.5%)	1. United Arab Emirates (126.0%)
136. Mozambique (97.3%)	153. Djibouti (105.0%)	132. Congo (Democratic Republic of the) (66.8%)	157. Senegal (88.7%)
137. Eritrea (97.0%)	154. Grenada (104.9%)	133. Angola (65.4%)	158. Nepal (87.8%)
138. India (97.0%)	155. India (104.7%)	134. India (65.2%)	159. India (87.7%)
139. Oman (96.9%)	156. China (104.7%)	135. Côte d'Ivoire (63.5%)	160. Morocco (87.5%)
140. Nigeria (96.9%)	157. Congo (104.7%)	136. Morocco (60.3%)	161. Korea (Republic of) (87.2%)
156. Yemen (92.7%)	194. Niger (96.9%)	152. Afghanistan (29.2%)	194. Afghanistan (55.3%)

Source : UNDP-women/Human Development Report, 2007-08—Country Fact Sheets—India.mht.

parliament, the percentage of female workers among professional and technical workers and the ratio of estimated female to male earned income (0.31).

EDUCATIONAL EMPOWERMENT OF INDIAN WOMEN

Gender inequality in education is decided by Percentage of female Adult literacy rate (47.8), Ratio of female to male adult literacy rate (0.65), female youth literacy rate (67.7), the ratio of female to male youth literacy rate (0.80), Net percentage of female primary enrolment rate (85), ratio of female to male net primary enrolment rate (0.93), Gross percentage of female primary enrolment ratio (116), Ratio of female to male gross primary enrolment ratio (0.94), Gross percentage of female secondary enrolment ratio (50%), ratio of female to male gross secondary enrolment ratio (0.80), Gross percentage of female tertiary enrolment ratio (9) and ratio of female to male gross tertiary enrolment ratio (0.70) in 2005.

ECONOMIC EMPOWERMENT OF INDIAN WOMEN

Gender inequality in economic activity is decided by Economic activity rate, female (% aged 15 and older) (34%), Economic activity index (1990=100), female (aged 15 and older) (94%), Economic activity rate (female rate as % of male rate, aged 15 and older), 2005 (42%), employment in agriculture, female (% of total female employment), Employment in agriculture, male (% of total male employment), Employment in industry, female (% of total female employment), Employment in industry, male (% of total male employment), Contributing family workers, men (% of total), 1995 2004 employment in services, female (% of total female employment) and contributing family workers, women (% of total).

Social Empowerment of Indian Women

The serious social evils like sati, ill treatment of widows and divorcees, ban on widow remarriage, dowry system, polygamy, child marriage, denial of property rights, denial of women education, temple prostitution, custom of purdah, abortion of girl babies, female infanticide, wife battering, bride burning, rape, abduction and sexual harassment are slowly reducing in India. But some of the problems still exist. The social status of 33 million widows representing 8 per cent of the total female population reveals a sad state of affairs. This has not attracted much research.

POLITICAL EMPOWERMENT OF INDIAN WOMEN

In 1950 Indian women received right to stand for election. In 1952, first woman elected (E) or appointed (A) to parliament. In 1950, Indian women received right to vote. In 2005, 3.4% women in government are at ministerial level (as % of total). In 1990, 5% seats of women in lower house or single house. In 2007, 8.3% of seats in lower house or single house are held by women. In 2007, 10.7% of seats in upper house or senate are held by women.

TABLE 5.3
Women in Parliament down the Decades

Parliament	*Year*	*Total seats*	*Women*	*Percentage*
1	1952-57	499	22	4.4
2	1957-62	500	27	5.4
3	1962-67	503	34	6.7
4	1967-71	523	31	5.9
5	1971-76	521	22	4.2
6	1977-80	544	19	3.4
7	1980-84	544	28	5.1
8	1985-90	544	44	8.1
9	1990-91	517	27	5.22

A country where there is more than 50 per cent women population, the power to represent themselves in decision making is just 4.4% to 7.4%. While having a glance at the above table, it is clearly noted that the number of seats occupied by women is comparatively low to men. This is because the number of educated men is high while the number of educated women is very less. Another reason is that women are not encouraged in various fields like politics, etc. Due of the lack of encouragement their interest turns to household work and dairy farming instead of books.

The above analysis shows us very clearly that Indian women are comparatively in a poor state of economic, social and political empowerment. The ranking of India in the Human Development Index, Gender Development Index and Gender Empowerment index speaks volumes about the real status of Indian women. Women form a significant proportion of our population and represent a source of untapped potential – a cause and consequence of our country's slow progress. India has a long history of women's welfare and rights. But still the position of Indian women is so worse in the world, that they are the sufferers compared to their counterparts. Governmental programs have been launched towards the empowerment of Indian women but effective and strict implementation will help us to achieve the desired goal.

6

Educational Status of Women in India

'If you educate a woman, you are educating a family. If you are educating all women, you are educating the whole world'.

India in its Globalisation era boasting about its Nuclear Power and Information Technology, cannot deny the harsh realities of poverty, unemployment, over population, hunger, illiteracy, etc. Food, water and shelter—the basic necessities are dreams alone for many. Higher Education is continuing to be a luxury even for the middle class. The dual status of men and women is continuing. The literacy gap among male and female is continuing to exist. Women's education in India plays a very important role in the overall development of the country. It not only helps in the development of half of the human resources, but in improving the quality of life at home and outside. Educated women not only tend to promote education of their girl children, but also can provide better guidance to all their children. Moreover, educated women can also help in the reduction of infant mortality rate and growth of the population.

Although in the Vedic period women had access to education in India, they had gradually lost this right. However, in the British period there was revival of interest in women's education in India. During this period, various socio-religious movements led by eminent persons like Raja Ram Mohan Roy, Iswar Chandra Vidyasagar emphasized on women's education in India. Mahatma Jyotiba Phule, Periyar and Baba Saheb Ambedkar were leaders of the lower castes in India who took various initiatives to make education available to the women of India. However, women's education got a fillip after the country got independence in 1947 and the government has taken various measures to provide education to all Indian women. As a result, women's literacy rate has grown over the three decades and the growth of female literacy has in fact been higher than that of male literacy rate. While in 1971 only 22% of Indian women were literate, by the end of 2001 54.16% female were literate. The growth of female literacy rate is 14.87% as compared to 11.72% of that of male literacy rate.

Though female literacy is gradually rising, the female literacy rate in India is lower than the male literacy rate. Compared to boys, far fewer girls are enrolled in the schools, and many of them drop out. According to the National Sample Survey Data of 1997, only the states of Kerala and Mizoram have approached universal female literacy rates. According to majority of the scholars, the major factor behind the improved social and economic status of women in Kerala is literacy. Under Non-Formal Education programme, about 40% of the centers in states and 10% of the centers in UTs are exclusively reserved for females. As of 2000, about 0.3 million NFE centers were catering to about 7.42 million children, out of which about 0.12 million were exclusively for girls. Currently, in engineering, medical and other colleges, 30% of the seats have been reserved for females. In urban india, girls are nearly at par with the boys in terms of education. However, in rural India girls continue to be less educated than the boys.

According to a 1998 report by U.S. Department of Commerce, the chief barrier to female education in India are inadequate school facilities (such as sanitary facilities), shortage of female teachers and gender bias in curriculum (majority of the female characters being depicted as weak and helpless).

In 2001, Indian male literacy rate was 75.96% whereas the female literacy was just 54.28 per cent. UNESCO defines a literate as one 'who can with understanding both read and write a short simple statement on his everyday life'. Considering the definition, this rate is a poor state of affair for any country. It is a well known fact that education is the foundation stone for the future economic and social development of any country. It is also a fact that 'If you educate a woman, you are educating a family'. In such a case, if we educate the female population, the whole country will be educated.

Considering Indian environment, constitutionally and legally women enjoy the unique status of equality with men. Women are given special reservations other than the open quota in many areas, including in the elections. Special tax deductions are permitted for women, so as to promote women employment. Priorities are given for the sprouting women's colleges and schools. We have separate women's universities and not men's. In sports, lesser standards are fixed for women. Special schemes and extra incentives are provided by the government of India for the development of women. Eighth of March is celebrated as the international women's day. The year 2001, was declared by the Indian government as the women's year. Innumerable women movements, women institutions and organisations are working hard for women empowerment and upliftment.

In spite of all the above attractions and incentives given for women, the female population ratio, the female literacy ratio, female employment ratio, female school or college enrolment ratio, etc., continue to be at a lower rate.

According to Mohan M. Mathew (2001), the Indian average female-male ratio (FMR) of 0.93 (2001 census) is the second lowest in the world (after Pakistan) lower than the FMR of sub-Saharan Africa. As per the reports of Sukumar Basu (2000), the percentage of female labour force compared to the total labour force is just 28.5 per cent in 1991. India is ranked 125th in the Gender Empowerment Index, as per the UNDP database.

Education is the basic tool to tap the 50 per cent potential of our human resource.

Oxford Dictionary defines the word education as 'training a person mentally and morally'. Starting from the Seargent plan of 1944, many efforts are taken by the government and other statutory organisations like UGC and NCERT to promote female literacy. Article 45 of the constitution emphasise compulsory universal education up to the age of 14 years. All five year plans are emphasising on education. In 1996, the Kothari Commission recommended that 6 per cent of the GDP be allocated for education. But, this has not materialised even today.

A comprehensive purpose of education is given by Dr. Adiseshiah (1972), 'The government should take steps to meet the increasing demand with adequate supply of educational services. 'It (education) must itself be a factor of social change and technological progress while continuing to transmit a cultural heritage. It must be more and more closely linked to preparation for an employment market where competition is ever more ruthless, training more diversified and specialized skills obsolete before they can be fully mastered. And it must reconcile the rapidly evolving social and economic requirements of society with the awakening aspirations of the individual. At the same time, education must continue to fulfil its age-old role: to build character; to combine and balance scientific and technological knowledge and training, and humanistic, ethical and cultural values; to help the student achieve an idea of purpose, a sense of underlying unity and permanence in the midst of extremities and accelerating change.

GENDER DIFFERENCES: CASTE-RELIGION INTERFACE

It needs to be recognized as given in the report of Dr. Sukhadeo Thorat (2008), that although the enrolment ratios are generally lower for the female compared to the male, the female belonging to the lower caste and some religious groups suffer more in access to higher education than others. For instance in 2000, as against the overall average of 9.4% for the female, the GER was 2.4% for ST female followed by 4.7% for SC female, 7.6% for OBC female and 17.2% for other female. Thus the GER for ST female was seven times less compare to the higher caste female. Similarly, the GER of the SC female was lower by about four times compared with higher caste female.

In the case of religious group, the Muslim women suffer the most. The GER of Muslim female was 6.3% compared to 10.8% for Hindu female, 12.7% for Sikh/Buddhist female, 20% for Christian and 48% for Jain female.

In the case of enrolment ratio for eligible (EER) the inter-caste disparities in the female are particularly significant. The EER for SC/OBC female was the lowest with about 50% compared to 57% for ST/other high caste female.

Similarly, the EER was the lowest for the Muslim female compared to the female belonging to other religion. The EER was 48% for Muslim female—about 54% for Hindu/Buddhist female, 56% for Sikh and about 69% for Jain/Christian female.

FEMALE DROPOUTS FROM EDUCATION

It is estimated that 45 per cent of girls drop out of schools between classes 1 and 5. Of the literate women in India, 59 percent have only a primary education or less. Only 41 percent of the literate population, or 13 percent of all Indian women, have more than a primary education. Although literacy levels are low, there has been progress in improving educational attainment in India over the last several decades. In 1971, only 22 percent of women and 46 percent of men were literate. By 1991, 39 percent of women and 64 percent of men were literate. Thus, there has been a large increase in the proportion of women who are literate in just 20 years. Despite the improvements in literacy, there continues to be a large gap between the literacy levels of men and of women. In 1991, the urban female literacy rate was more than twice that of the rural rate, 64 and 31 percent, respectively

AREA-WISE MALE-FEMALE LITERACY GAP

The following table shows the percentage of literacy among men and women among various types of areas.

In villages, the literacy gender gap is very high, whereas in cities it is not so. In tribal areas the literacy gap is extremely wider among men and woman.

The bar diagram and the table shows clearly that Indian literacy rate is going on increasing. But the female literacy rate

TABLE 6.1
Area-wise Male-female Literacy Gap in 1991

Place/Status	*Men*	*Women*
Cities	81.09%	64.05%
Villages	57.87%	30.62%
Scheduled	49.91%	23.76%
Tribal	40.67%	18.19%

Source : Women's links, Cyril & Co., Human Rights Education, Vaigarai Publishing.

TABLE 6.2
Literacy Gap between 1950-51 to 2000-01

Year	*Male literacy*	*Female Literacy*	*Total Literacy*
1950-51	27.16	8.86	18.33
1960-61	40.40	15.35	28.3
1970-71	45.96	21.97	34.45
1980-81	56.38	29.76	43.57
1990-91	64.1	39.3	52.2
2000-01	75.85	54.16	65.38

Source :www.indiabudget.nic.in

CHART 6.1
Male-Female Literacy Gap in India from 1950-51 to 2000-01

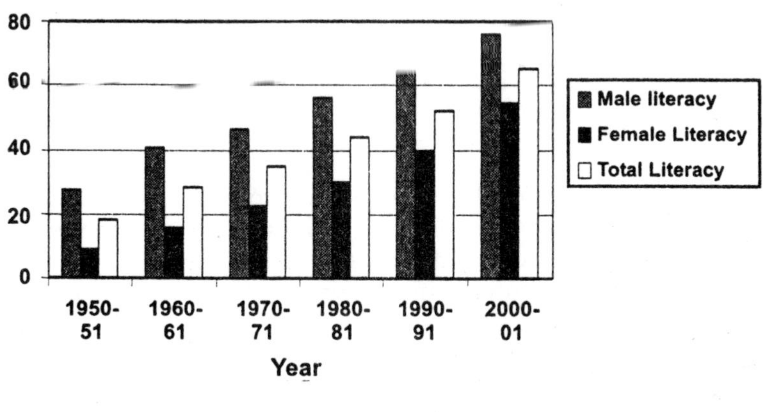

is the lowest in all the period. It is also below the total literacy rate.

RELATIONSHIP BETWEEN LITERACY AND OTHER FACTORS DECIDING WOMEN EMPOWERMENT

An analysis is done to relate the female literacy with few other indicators of women empowerment. Female literacy, female sex ratio, female work participation and female enrolment at university level are considered as the index of women's positive growth position. The percentage of women suffering from anaemia, female drop outs and crimes against women are the indicators of women oppression. The variables in the table were correlated with the literacy rate to find out the degree in which literacy affect these factors and to prove that literacy could only be the targeted solution for women empowerment. The results are as follows:

TABLE 6.3
Correlation between Literacy and Other Factors Deciding Women Empowerment in India

Relationship between Literacy and other factors	*Correlation*
Literacy and Female sex ratio	0.401
Literacy and Female work participation	0.113
Literacy and Female enrolment at university	0.743**
Literacy and Percentage of women with anaemia	-0.565**
Literacy and Female dropout rate	-0.537**
Literacy and Crime rate against women	0.093

* Significant at 5 per cent level.
** Significant at one per cent level.

Female sex ratio in the population is correlated with female literacy at a co-efficient of 0.401. The literacy and female work participation rate are correlated at a co-efficient of 0.113. The literacy and female enrolment at university level are correlated positively with a co-efficient of 0.743.** And hence female literacy surely improves the female work participation, female sex ratio and female enrolment at university level. In other words the states having more literacy are having better female work participation, female sex ratio and female enrolment at university level.

And it is also proved that literacy and percentage of women with anaemia are correlated at a rate of –0.565 with 1% level of significance and literacy and Female dropout rate are correlated a rate of –0.537 and is significant at 1% level. Therefore, female literacy reduces percentage of women with anaemia and female dropouts though not much of crime rates.

It is paradoxical to see that, the crime rate against women does not have any relation with literacy. The correlation between literacy and crime rate against women is nearing zero that is 0.093. So whether the women are educated or not, they are exploited by the society. Educated women suffer in a different way and uneducated suffer in a different way. The reason could also be that the women become more aware of their rights and hence their sufferings are brought to any platform for discussion.

The literate states have proved themselves with more female population ratio, more female work participation, and more enrolment for higher education, good health records and less female drop outs. And hence the literacy could only be the solution for women empowerment.

Factors responsible for the slow growth of woman and woman literacy:

In the process of development, the contribution of women towards the growth of the country is ever increasing. But their social status, educational status, economic status and political status continue to remain below their counterparts. The lower status of women in the society does not give them confidence to come out of their shells. Hence it is necessary to identify the factors responsible for this serious issue.

Our cultural history and Political history has proved that women were considered as a secondary human being. It is considered that the birth of a son is bliss incarnate, while that of a daughter is the root of family misery. Only the sons are the heirs of their parents and they are eligible to do the final rites of their parents.

Social Constraints

The serious social evils like sati, ill treatment of widows and divorcees, ban on widow remarriage, dowry system, polygamy, child marriage, denial of property rights, denial of women education, temple prostitution, custom of purdah, abortion of girl babies, female infanticide, wife battering, bride burning, rape, abduction and sexual harassment are the special unpleasant features of Indian women's social environment. These serious evils do not permit them to come out for education

Women with higher qualification and higher earnings are generally secluded from their society. The social practice of marrying highly qualified and highly earning bridegroom discourages the parents to permit their girl children for education. The overall Indian social structure which constitutes religion, caste, custom, tradition, culture, family structure and other social institutions remind every one that woman is inferior.

The naturality of child birth and child rearing makes women's life hectic. The psychological trauma and the physical pains undergone during the menstruation, menopause and child birth, etc. are constraints for the women to flourish. The diseases associated in all these process also add to the trauma. Pregnant Indian women have the world's highest levels of anaemia. Child psychology books say that girls mental I.Q level is high when compared to boys up to the age of 10 to 12. After 10 to 12 the boys I.Q. exceeds girls I.Q. This may be due to the natural constraints.

Unpleasant School Atmosphere

The pattern of education is promoting rote learning, where there is less scope for overall personality dovelopment. The curriculum does not permit us to use the full potentials of the students. Children, especially the rural children lack encouragement and support from the school. Their creativity is not encouraged. Corporal punishment given by the teachers is one of the major reasons for drop-outs and child labour is this practice. Inefficient Teachers does not promote the creativity and self-confidence of the students by their attitude and words.

If education is made more attractive, drop outs will be reduced considerably. Many of the rural schools could not provide water, toilet and such facilities for the girls. Due to these basic reasons, there are heavy drop outs among girls. There is less awareness about the schemes, scholarships, financial incentives and programmes available for women.

Ragging and Eve Teasing are the major problems faced by female children, while going for education.

The role conflict of the women also makes them psychologically inferior. Women have to play a dual role if they opt for career life. Priority cannot be given for any of these roles. And hence the psychological and emotional pressures lead to lots of trauma.

The most conspicuous failure of the Indian Educational system is that it has failed to implement the directive of Article 45 of the Constitution which had recommended that the state should provide free and compulsory education for all children until they complete the age of 14 years by 1960. Political priorities and defence priorities overpower the educational priorities in financial resource allocation. If this is made a reality, there is no question of female literacy.

India and China put together form 2/5 or 40 per cent of the world population. In 1950, India's literacy level in the age group of 16-40 was 16 per cent while of China was 20 per cent where as India's literacy rate stands at 36 per cent in 1981 and that of China was 66 per cent in the same year.

If the current situation continues, India will have to face a gloomy future. Till we reach the day of compulsory primary education, we cannot imagine a bright future for Indian women. To quote Jawaharlal Nehru, "The level of democracy in a country, thus can be measured by the standard of education of its residents". To conclude, a good social environment has to be enabled by the government to promote women to participate in various fields. More efforts should be taken to bring about good self development among women right from their childhood.

7

Status of Women Scientists in India

"It is impossible to think about the welfare of the world unless the condition of women is improved. It is possible for a bird to fly on only one wing?"

—Swami Vivekananda

By the dawn of 20th century, women become more aware of their social position and started utilizing their potential. Hence there is a substantial rise in their development. In some fields they even supersede men. The performance of girls in class X and Class XII examinations is always much better than that of boys in all subjects. The scientific advancement shows the level of development among any particular group.

Women scientists have been there since time immemorial. The first literature appeared some 4,000 years ago. Stone and bone records stretch back further than those first alphabets, but give us no names. The very first technical name was male—Imhotep—the architect of the first pyramid. The second technical name was female—En Hedu' Anna (c. 2534 BCE). Women have been physicians in great numbers ever since there have been women. Midwifery was almost exclusively run by women until the 19th century.

Women have achieved a lot in Astronomy. The first Harvard Ph.D. award for Astronomy was given to a woman, Cecillia Payne-Gasposchkin in 1925. In the 1920's women earned almost 27% of all astronomy doctorates awarded by U.S. Universities which was the highest in any science field. Even though she has contributed quality work in Science like discoveries, which includes the discovery of galaxy, comets and orbits, they have not received any significant recognition. Their men colleagues have been recognized for their equal or lesser contribution to science.

Maria Mitchel, an astronomer was the first U.S. woman to receive recognition in science. She had learned from her father how to use a telescope, to study the sky and to calculate the orbits. In 1847, at the age of 29, she discovered a comet, and received a gold medal from the king of Denmark. By 1871, 18 of the women's academies had observatories and offered a course in Astronomy. Between 1877 to 1919, 45 women were employed at the Harvard college observatory. Caroline Herschel (1750-1848), was an astronomer and mathematician from Germany. She discovered the Andromeda and the Cetus nebulae. When she was 85 years old, the Royal Astronomical society of England elected her as an honorary member, an honour that she and Mary Somerville were the first women to receive. Mary Fairfax Somerville (1780-1872) from England mastered Astronomy and Newton's Principia. She has published her papers in the field of Physical Science, Physical Geography, Molecular and Microscopic Science. Mary Curie (1867-1934) was the women Scientist well recognized and a two time noble laureate for her work on radioactivity. She discovered two elements—radium and polonium. To honour her, one of the elements in the periodic table of elements in named after her "Curium". Her daughter Irene Joliot Curie also received the Nobel Prize in 1935 for her work on artificial radioactivity. Annie Jump Cannon, was awarded the first honorary degree ever bestowed on a woman by Oxford University. Most of the men scientists were ably helped by their wives who contributed their best behind the screen to fetch fame for their husbands. It should be mentioned that the first X-ray was the picture of Mrs. Rongen, wife of Rongen who received the Nobel Prize for this discovery.

The impedance for vertical growth of women in modern professions does not lie in their poor academic achievement or in their lack of interest. It is merely rooted in the overall social structure, where women have been assigned inferior positions and also her roles are strictly defined and prescribed. Invariably in all fields both in developed and developing countries women potential is not tapped fully.

TABLE 7.1
Women's Earning as a Percentage of Men's in USA

Year	*Percentage*
1951	63.9
1961	59.2
1971	59.5
1981	59.2
1991	69.9
2001	76.0
2002	76.0

Source : US Women's Bureau and the National.

COMMITTEE ON PAY EQUITY, AMANAC 2004—TIME

The Table 7.1 shows clearly that till today the women of even a developed countries have not got their equal share with men.

Since 1901, there have been over three hundred recipients of the Noble Prize in the Sciences, only ten of them (3 per cent) are women.

Now let us have a look out on women scientists in India.

The total number of women as fellows of National Science Academies in 17 (6.7 percent), the male outnumber them by 236 (93.3 percent).

An effort was taken to consider the percentage of women scientists in India, for which Anjana Chattopadhyay's "Biographical Dictionary of Indian Scientists, 2002 was taken into consideration". This book presents the sketch of 2063 scientists, out of which only 62 are women (3 percent).

TABLE 7.2
Percent of Women Scientists in Research Institutions in India

Agency	*Institutions*	*Male*	*Female*	*Percentage of Female*
DBT	DBT	23	2	8
DBT	NII	18	1	5
CSIR	CDRI	11	1	18
CSIR	CCMB	10	0	0
ICMR	NIN	20	3	13
ICMR	NICED	15	4	21

The above table clearly shows the percentage of women scientist in advisory committees of Department of Biotechnology (DBT), National Institute of Immunology, New Delhi (NII), Central Drug Research Institute, Lucknow (CDRI), Centre for Cellular and Molecular Biology (CCMB), Hyderabad National Institute of Nutrition, Hyderabad (NIN) and National Institute for Cholera and Enteric Diseases, Kolkata (NICED) which are funded by Department of Bio-technology Council of Scientific and Industrial Research, Indian Council for Medical Research (ICMR) does not give equal representation for women. In the above reference the ratio of women in research advisory committee is only 11 compared to 97 of men.

Other than the institutes considered, in the above Table 7.2, some more institutes like Advanced Centre for Treatment, Research and Education in Cancer, Mumbai (ACTREC), National Centre for Cell Science (NCCS), Bose Institute and Agharkar Institute, etc., were also included for studying the proportion of women faculty members.

The Table 7.3 proves that the percentage of women faculty is on an average from 20 to 31 per cent except for ACTREC where there is 54.5 percent of female faculty.

Another example is also given below to prove that women scientists are very less in number in reputed institutes and universities.

TABLE 7.3

Proportion of Women Faculty Members in a Few National Institutions Funded by Government

Funding Agency	*Institute*	*Total No. of Faculty*	*Women (Percent)*
CSIR	CDRI	193	46(23.8)
CSIR	CCMB	70	22(31.4)
DAE	ACTREC	33	18(54.5)
DBT	NII	38	9(23.7)
DBT	NCCS	25	5(20.0)
DST	Bose Institute	61	14(23.0)
DST	Agharkar Institute	39	12(30.8)
ICMR	NIN	48	15(31.2)
ICMR	NICED	33	7(21.2)

Source : Vineeta Bal, Women Scientists in India, *EPW*, Aug. 7, 2004.

TABLE 7.4

Women Faculty as per cent of Total Faculty

Institutes	*Total Faculty*	*No. of Women*	*Women (Percent)*
IIT Kharagpur	404	17	4.2
IIT Delhi	333	25	7.5
University of Roorkee	321	22	6.8
Jadavpur University	516	45	8.7
Total	1574	109	6.9

Source : Namrata Gupta and Sharma—Triple Burden among Women Scientists in India.

Table 7.4 shows the strength of women faculty at institutes/universities. The number of women faculty in the institutes is only 6.9 percent, which is very low.

The slow growth of women scientists attracted the attention of Indian National Science Academy (INSA) to attempt a study on women scientists with the help of a nine number committee. They found that girls are highly interested in science subjects. The parents also never discourage them because the science students find good place in the marriage market. Yet when it comes to careers in science, the number suddenly drops. The reasons attributed are poor transport system, necessity to stay back in work field for long hours, marriage of the women, sexual harassment at the work place and other gender-related harassments.

To improve the women participation in science, institutions offering science education have major responsibility. Knowing fully well the problem of women the education system should change their syllabus and pattern of study to suit their varying needs. Flexi hours of quality education can be thought about.

The UNESCO manual on rural women technology prepared by the centre of science for villagers can be of great use.

Retarding Forces

The income discrimination, promotion discrimination and sexual harassments are assigned as main reasons for the lower contribution of women in Science. There are few reported cases of sexual harassment in both academic and research environment. Many women are forced to quite their challenging position due to this problem. Some men use it as a weapon to keep women out of their career. Children should be educated at their school level to treat the opposite sex with due respect and this alone can establish a healthy academic and research atmosphere conductive for women to concentrate in their work.

The subordination of women is deeply rooted in the conscience of both men and women. Women are expected to go for shorter training periods to enable their parents to get them married since it is considered to be ultimate achievement for a girl. Women who successfully cross such odds and come to scientific professions also suffer due to the roles they are expected to play in the society. The women have to balance domestic management and the scientific work leading to severe mental stress and feeling of insufficiency to cope up with scientific advancement. Hence, many such women are forced to take up a new job to suit their family commitments at the expense of their scientific fervour.

SUGGESTIONS TO IMPROVE PARTICIPATION IN SCIENCE

Serious efforts should be taken to pool the potentials of women towards scientific achievements.

- An integrated effort should be taken towards all the schemes of state government and central government.
- Leadership qualities in women should be developed to enhance their confidence level.
- Steps should be taken to make science subjects more attractive. Faculty recruitments are more based on improper methodologies; the teachers are not able to make the subjects interesting. The brilliant brains of the schools directly enter into any of the professional courses. Hence the faculties, who come out of the left over, drain the whole beauty of the subjects.
- School teachers are not paid well, when compared to higher education faculty and hence there is not much attraction.
- The college fee for science (including laboratory fees) is high when compared to arts and hence the brilliant poor children hesitate to choose science.
- Awareness programmes should become an essential feature for parents and students to help them realize the importance of science. Teachers in schools and colleges should be given enough exposure so that they can motivate their students. School teachers must work in coordination with college teachers who should have collaboration with universities and research centres.
- The publications of research findings are very important. But the women scientists, who publish also should publish papers on the methodology by which they overcome the difficulties. They must also publish articles to create awareness among the general public.
- Young women should be motivated through mentors and supervisors to help them overcome the barriers at various stages.
- Universities and Research Centres must guarantee transparent and fair mechanisms of recruitment.

Heavy corruption in recruitment process destroys the whole process of merit. One crore to 5 crore for Vice-chancellor and many lakhs for lecturers and professors posts. In most of the places women are not involved in such illegal activities, and hence they are not able to enter into such positions.

- Women scientists should be identified and they should be publicized as role models. They should be invited as speakers for meetings and conferences.
- Awards of government funds should be given only to organizations and institutions that make gender equality.
- Every educational and research institutions must provide a family friendly environment, which will facilitate women to show quality output.

The scientific contributions of any community show the level of development. And hence the women potential should not be left out.

8

Status of Female Aged Population in India

Advances in medical services, health, nourishment, improved standards of public health have all contributed to the lengthening of human life. The population of Senior Citizen and its ratio to the total population has been increasing rapidly in both developed and developing countries. There is nothing surprising about this increase. The census has predicted the need to make provision not only for the present aging population but also for that of the future. The developed world has been facing the problem of looking after its growing number of Senior Citizens taking affective measures to cope with it. The seriousness of this problem so far, however, has hardly been noticed in developing countries. Special privileges were announced in the recent budget shows the realization of this importance.

Old age is really a social category that is defined differently by various cultures. Age 62 is the age at which person can take "Early Retirement". Age 65 has been the traditional age for full retirement. However because of longer life expectations the full retirement age is increasing. For people born after 1938 full retirement age is going from 65 to 67.

The statistics in India reveal that there has been a marked increase in the number of elderly persons in the past few decades. In India persons above sixty years of age are classified as aged persons. In India there were only 12 million people but it increased to 19 Million in 1951. In 2001 it became 77 Million. The rapid increase in the population of older persons can be attributed to the following factors:

- Advancements in medical health/technologies
- Gradual fall in mortality rate
- Increased awareness
- Better nutrition
- Increased life expectancy

While the numbers have gone up, the quality of life led by the older persons has gone down. Many elderly find it difficult to adjust in their own homes due to intergeneration gaps, varying attitudes, varying perceptions, thoughts and feelings.

GROWTH OF MALE AND FEMALE OLD AGE PEOPLE IN INDIA

The growth of old ageing in India and the composition of male and female are shown in Table 8.1 for the data for elderly between 1951 and 2001. Based on trend analysis the data are projected.

TABLE 8.1

Growth of 60+ Population in India : 1951 to 2021

Year	*Total (in mill.)*	*Male (in mill.)*	*Female (in mill.)*
1951	19.6	9.7	9.9
1961	24.7	12.4	12.4
1971	32.7	16.9	15.8
1981	43.2	22.0	21.1
1991	56.7	29.4	27.3
2001	70.9	36.4	34.5
Projected values			
2011	77.60	40.09	37.51
2021	87.97	45.5	42.46

The above table explains that the 60+ women population is higher than the men population in first two decades after 1950, (i.e.) 1951 and 1961. After that the men population above 60 is higher than women population. The total number of 60+ population is increasing year by year at a rate of 70 to 80 percent. It is because of increasing life span and life expectancy due to medical advancement. The male and female 60+ population is also increasing with less difference in percentage (around 1% to 5%). The population of the elderly in India has doubled in the last 25 years. The table above depicts the increase in the number of elderly over the last century.

GROWTH IN THE MALE AND FEMALE AGED POPULATION TO THE TOTAL AGED POPULATION

India is witnessing a silent demographic revolution due to steady growth of its population. While in terms of percentage the overall population has grown by 170 percent since 1947 that of the '60 plus' category is growing at an alarming rate of 270 percent due to reduction in birth rate and increase in life

TABLE 8.2
The Proportion of the Aged Male and Female Population

Year	*Aged Population Male (%)*	*Percentage to Total (%)*	*Aged male Percentage to Total Male (%)*	*Aged Female Percentage to Total Female (%)*
1901	12.06	5.06	4.55	5.59
1911	12.17	5.22	4.81	5.65
1921	13.48	5.37	5.04	5.70
1931	14.21	5.09	4.86	5.35
1941	18.04	5.06	5.43	5.91
1951	19.61	5.43	5.21	5.66
1961	24.17	5.63	5.46	5.80
1971	32.70	5.79	5.94	5.99
1981	43.73	6.42	6.35	6.50
1991	55.30	6.75	6.45	6.60
2001	75.93	7.70	7.55	7.86

population of elderly. The number has touched 75.9 million by 2001. India ranks fourth in terms of Aged Population second only to China.

This analysis shows that the Aged Female Percentage to Total female (%) is high in India when compared to the Aged male Percentage to Total Male (%). It is also clear that the aged population is growing at a faster rate and hence special plans should be adopted for old people.

Though government is providing some special treatment for Senior citizens, the facilities are not enough. Effective plans are needed for meeting the growing elderly population. Discriminated and exclusive policies are needed for male and female Senior citizens and for various states. Finally, aged should be considered as a valuable cultural resources and role models for the younger generation. Therefore, government and non-government organizations should come forward to motivate and create awareness among the youth to take the care of the aged in the family. In the words of Addison, Joseph, "He who would pass his decline years that he may one day become old, and remember when he is old, that he has once been young".

9

Women Entrepreneurship in India

'Gender equality is critical to the development and peace of every nation.'
—Kofi Annan

Industrial development is said to be the major component of economic development and industrial development envisages entrepreneurial development. Entrepreneurial development is leading to industrial development and the later leading to economic development. Hence this mutual interdependence is the root that necessitates the entrepreneurial development. In India, for instance, according to the 1981 census, there are as many as 935 women for every 1000 men—the women's share in employment is only 21 per cent. And when we imagine the entrepreneurial activities among the women, it is very meager and insignificant. It is unjust to leave the 50% potential of the human resource untapped. This study aims at identifying the entrepreneurial capacities in Madurai so that it will help us to find whether the full potential is used.

Women entrepreneurs may be defined as a women or groups of women who initiate, organize and run a business enterprise. R.B.I. defines, women Enterprise as a small industrial unit/industry related service or business enterprise managed by one or more women entrepreneurs in proprietary concerns or in which she/they individually or jointly have a share capital of not less than 51% as partners/share holders/directors of the private limited company/members of co-operative society. *According to Government of India,* 'a women entrepreneur is defined as an enterprise owned and controlled by a women having a minimum financial interest of 51 per cent of the capital and giving at least 51 per cent of the employment generated in the enterprise to women'. In short, women entrepreneurs are those women who think of a business enterprise, initiate it, organize and combine the factors of production, operate the enterprise and undertake risks and handle economic uncertainty involved in running a business enterprise.

In the traditional Indian Society, women are generally accorded in inferior social status. The leadership potentials of women is basically very high, when compared to men. But the potentials are hidden by the social, economic and political constraints. By the dawn of 20th century women become more aware of their social position and started utilising their potential. Hence there is a substantial rise in their development.

When the women use their enterprising capacity, they will become they will be treated justfully in the society. Economic empowerment leads to women empowerment. Entrepreneurship is a method of making the women, who otherwise remain unemployed, to participate in the development process. Entrepreneurship is a powerful tool to provide employment in the economy. Entrepreneur is one who identifies opportunities and seizes opportunities mainly for economic gains. Entrepreneurs are basically individuals who are ready to take risk.

Self Help Group women play a significant and crucial role in taking up various activities like dairy, poultry, horticulture, food processing, garments, handicraft, fisheries, departmental stores, etc. and they are responsible for more than half of the world production from community based enterprises. Most women remain deprived of employment opportunities as wage workers because of their family responsibilities, social and cultural barriers. In this context, self-employment or setting up enterprises of their own may become an opportunity for women, to get an income and to acquire financial security. Taking up such a venture in the form of micro enterprises will also play a major role for improving the economic development of the country.

SIGNIFICANCE OF WOMEN ENTREPRENEURSHIP

- The entrepreneurship plays a major role in the economic development of an economy.
- Entrepreneurship promotes increase in national production and productivity in the primary, secondary and tertiary sectors through technical and other forms of innovation.
- It promotes capital formation by mobilizing the idle saving of the public.
- It provides immediate large-scale employment. Thus it helps to reduce the unemployment and under employment problems in the country.
- It facilitates the transfer of technology.
- It promotes balanced regional development.
- It helps in dispersal of economic power.
- It stimulates the equitable redistribution of wealth, income and political power in the interest of the country.
- It also induces backward and forward linkages which stimulate the process of economic development in the country.
- It also promotes country's export trade.

GROWTH AND DEVELOPMENT OF WOMEN ENTREPRENEURS

Women in India contribute around half of the country's population. Hence, they are regarded as the 'better half of the society'. Emergence and development of entrepreneurship is largely caused by the availability of supporting conditions in a country. With the improving supporting conditions, the share of women owned enterprises in the United States has risen from

7.1% in 1977 to 32% in 1990. It is likely to reach to 50% by the turn of the present century.

Women in India plunged into business for both pull and push factors. Pull factors imply the factors which encourage women to start an occupation or venture with an urge to do something independently. Push factors refer to those factors which compel women to take up their own business to tide over their economic difficulties and responsibilities.

Encouragement from family members Earning money, Independence, Govt. incentives and concessions, Time passing, No other job, Self-interest education and training received and social status are generally the motivating factors of women entrepreneurs.

With growing awareness about business and spread of education among women over the period, women have started shifting from 3 Ps viz., Pickles, Powder and Pappad to engross to 3 modern Es viz., Engineering, Electronics and Energy.

There are three types of business activities viz., Manufacturing, Trading and Servicing. In the manufacturing sector, women were involved in preparation of appalam , cement tiles, grill work, sambrani, soap, pickle, masala powder and furniture. The women, who were involved in trading was involved in saree business, tiffin center, grocery shop, fancy store, medical shop, milk agent, rice business, edible oil, cool drinks, electricals, cycle spareparts business, etc. Under servicing sector women were involved in beauty parlour, tailoring, book binding, STD booth, DTP, photocopying, etc.

WOMEN'S ECONOMIC CONTRIBUTION AND VARIOUS SCHOOLS OF THOUGHT

There are three leading approaches to women's study. The principal elements of economic discussion are employment, occupational division of labour, wages, on-job mobility, access to education, training, division of invisible work and intra-household disparity. The aim of the theories is to explain the existing status of women with respect to these factors.

The neoclassical school of thought, which is also the most dominant school in the West, bases its explanation on the concept of utility. Human beings follow a rational behaviour and exercise their choice to maximise their utility, subject to incomes and prices. Women's participation in labour force is a function of the total (dis)utility derived out of market work, leisure and homework. If the price of market work goes up, with other things given constant, the labour force participation rises. However, if the household income (meaning husband's income) rises then the relative dis-utility of work increases and women tend to withdraw from the labour force. These are the inducing and non-inducing factors which determine the participation or withdrawal of women from the labour force.

The 'neo home-economics' which is the model of household behaviour in the neoclassical theory explains marriage as a relationship between individuals to maximise utility. Marriage is considered as a two-person firm with other members being an entrepreneur who hires the other at a salary and receives profits. Women hire men since the latter earn more and men hire women because they are superior nursemaids.

The third school of thought, namely, the Marxist school takes a historical view of any social situation. There are two streams of thought here. The first views women's position within the process of capital accumulation and class struggle. The second school, also referred to as Marxist Feminist School, understands history as a system of relations between men (Patriarchy) and women who are dominated. The Marxism in this approach takes the form of rooting patriarchy in the material base rather than the psychic one, and thereby claiming to eradicate the sex blindness of Marxist categories. The Marxist Feminist School has developed its formulation as if in vengeance against the male dominated society.

Whatever is the type of acceptance or contribution from women entrepreneurs, this issue of women participation in work is very important. According to Swarankar (1988), the magnitude of female participation in work force primarily depends upon:

1. The status the women enjoy in their family.
2. Economic exigency necessitating their participation in work.
3. Availability of suitable jobs.
4. Degree of consciousness to avail of the opportunities at hand and claim for their share.

5. Enhancing the standard of living by earnings and extra income.
6. Personal satisfaction, self-actualization, development and unfold of talents.
7. Utilization and justification of education and training.
8. Utilization of leisure in gainful employment.

WOMEN ENTREPRENEURS IN DISTRICTS OF TAMILNADU

Tamilnadu is in the Southern most part of India. In this analysis the variations in the growth of women entrepreneurs is studied.

TABLE 9.1
Women Entrepreneurs in Districts of Tamilnadu

Districts	*Number of Women Entrepreneurs*	*Rank*	*Percentage to total*
Chengai MGR	249	8	3.84
Coimbatore	1862	1	28.70
Dharmapuri	245	9	3.78
Dindigul Anna	146	12	2.25
Kamarajar	371	4	5.72
Kanyakumari	57	20	0.88
Madras	1176	2	18.13
Madurai	294	5	4.53
Nilgiris	94	15	1.45
North Arcot	285	6	4.53
Pasumpom Thevar Thirumagam	59	19	0.91
Periyar	215	11	3.31
Pudukkottai	224	10	3.45
Ramanathapuram	57	20	0.88
Salem	181	13	2.79
South Arcot	260	7	4.01
Tanjavur	405	3	6.24
Thirunelveli	60	18	0.92
Trichy	176	16	2.71
V.O.C.	72	17	1.11
Total	6488		100

Source: Women Entrepreneurs Directory, Directorate of Industries and Commerce, Madras, 2003.

The foregoing Table shows us clearly that Coimbatore and Madras are the toppers with maximum number of women entrepreneurs. While a short analysis of Descriptive statistics is done, the results derived were as follows:

Descriptive Statistics

N	*Minimum*	*Maximum*	*Mean*	*Std. Deviation*
20	57.00	1862.00	324.4000	436.0902

The mean value is 324.4, whereas the maximum number of women entrepreneurs was 1862 and the minimum number of women entrepreneurs was just 57. This is expressed in terms of the standard deviation 436.09. This means there is heavy variation among various districts of Tamilnadu. All districts are not equally grown in promoting women entrepreneurs. And hence the backward states should be given importance.

While a bi-variate correlation is applied, it was found out that the growth of Indian women entrepreneurs and Tamilnadu entrepreneurs are in inverse direction. The correlation showed that the relationship was –0.514

While the curve fit was found for the data available for the women entrepreneurs in India and Tamilnadu, the following results were derived. This was tried by having the years as independent variable and Number of women entrepreneneurs in India and Tamilnadu as the dependent variables.

Variables	*Rsq*	*F*	*Sig*	B_0	B_1
India	.397	5.26	051	1545.67	-38.485
Tamilnadu	.632	13.75	.006	10.4667	29.6606

The above analysis helps us to project the future. Anyhow it is surprising to know that the there is declining growth of women entrepreneurs in India and increasing growth of women entrepreneurs in Tamilnadu.

PROBLEMS OF WOMEN ENTREPRENEURS

Women Entrepreneurs face serious problems which are very difficult to be tackled by the government.

Mobilization of Fund

Mobilization of money for the investment is the first and foremost step for any entrepreneurship. Indian women does not have property rights from their parents and hence they are not able to mobilize money immediately. Women also do not have property in their names to use them as collateral for obtaining funds from external sources. Again banks and financial institutions consider women as less creditworthy and discourage their borrowing. And hence the Indian women entrepreneurs suffer from lack of finance for their business.

Survival during the Competition

Generally all entrepreneurs have to face competition throughout the whole lifecycle process of the business. But the women entrepreneurs face serious competition from their male counterparts. Women entrepreneurs do not have organizational set-up to pump in a lot of money for canvassing and advertisement.

Poor Education among Women

Prevailing serious illiteracy is the major reason why the women could not have any theoretical knowledge background of business. While setting up industries, lack of knowledge, leads to lags in administration. Without updated technology, one cannot face the technological competition from their business counter-parts.

Constraints of Mobility

Women are less mobile when compared to men. Since child birth and child rearing becomes the priority role for every married woman, they find it hard to move from one place to another place. Many social reasons also become responsible for their lack of mobility.

Natural Constraints

Women being the instrument of God for creation have to taken up the major chunk of family responsibilities. The regular physical pains of childbirth, menstrual pain and the menopause pain also push them down. In India, women takes the responsibilities of taking care of their husband, children, Parents, in-Laws, Grand parents and other members of the family.

Family Dependencies

In Indian families men are considered as the head of their families. And hence, when there is an opposition from their in-law side or husband side, women are forced to withdraw themselves from their adventurous tasks.

Equality among men and women becomes a priority consideration for any discussion. Unfortunately in practice it is the least consideration. Women are not treated as equal with men. Women are looked down upon as weak in all respects. They suffer from discrimination. This, in turn, serves as a barrier to women's entry into business.

To conclude, now-a-days, women are increasingly participating in all spheres of activities. The general consensus is that women entrepreneurs should form an integral part of all the developmental strategies of the government. Because entrepreneurship is the major instrument for absorbing the women potential towards economic development. Several national and international organizations and agencies have appreciated the need for and importance of developing women entrepreneurs in recent years.

10

Women Empowerment through Self Help Groups

Self Help Groups are the self-Governed, peer-controlled informal group of people with similar socio-economic background, having a desire to come forward voluntarily for a mutual agreement of helping each other for productive or consumptive purposes.

Though the SHG is a common activity, generally in most of the cases just one person takes the initiative. The potential members of the community are generally invited to join. But the group elects leaders democratically and conducts meetings.

Self Help Group concept is the brainchild of Grameen Bank of Bangladesh, which was founded by Prof. Mohammed Yunus of Chittagong University in the year 1975. The Self Help Group concept has got a mushrooming growth in various parts of the world in different forms.

In India, Self Help Groups (DWCRA groups) are the sub-schemes of Integrated Rural Development Scheme (I.R.D.P.) started in the year 1982-83. The main aim of the scheme is to bring together the women members of rural families living below the poverty line with a view to generate self-employment on sustainable basis.

In India, the Self Help Groups are working under three major drives: they are self-driven Self Help Groups, Government driven Self Help Groups and Non-Governmental Organisation's (NGOs—voluntary agencies including many Catholic churches) driven Self Help Groups. The NGO driven mechanism is comparatively functioning very effectively. The motivation levels of NGOs are comparatively higher because of their efforts of survival. But it is also true that not all NGOs are sincere in their tasks, because for such NGOs, social outlook becomes secondary.

FORMATION OF SELF HELP GROUPS

Generally one person takes the initiative of starting a Self Help Group. Interested people are motivated to join the team after clarifying the activities and mutual benefits. More likeminded members are promoted to come together for a common cause. Democratic elections are conducted to elect their leaders. Meetings are called on at regular intervals. Size of each group ranges from 12 to 20. N.G.O.s are generally the steering instruments and motivating factors of these groups.

ACTIVITIES OF SELF HELP GROUPS

- Create a common fund through their regular savings
- Organizing adult education centers
- Organizing Mahila Mandals and Youth Clubs
- Organizing balwadis
- Renewing the work of Jana Shiksha Nilayam, center for peoples' education
- Promoting Self Help Groups and their members
- To promote themselves in Economic Activities
- To help women in leadership position

Mechanism of Operation

The methodology behind Self Help Groups is collective wisdom of the poor and the collective organizational capabilities.

Peer Pressure: Financial Institutions use social collateral in the form of peer groups to ensure loan repayment. The peer pressure encourages borrowers to be very selective about their peer group members and to repay loans in full and on time.

Peer Group Monitoring: The group members have an incentive to monitor one another to ensure timely repayment of the loan.

Mobilization of Saving: The Self Help Groups encourages group savings as collateral substitute of the loan.

Voluntary Formation of the Group: The groups are voluntarily formed by the borrowers. Use of self-selected groups of borrowers, generally consist of a minimum of five members, who guarantee each other's loan.

Joint Liability: The joint liability concept means that SHGs should be formed of likeminded people who would voluntarily take up joint liability for the group/individual loans.

Progress of SHGs and their Bank Loans in India and Tamil Nadu

Year	*India*		*Tamil Nadu*	
	No. of SHGs	*Bank Loan (in Lakhs)*	*No. of SHGs*	*Bank Loan (Rs. In Lakhs)*
1992-93	255	3	22	2.239
1993-94	620	7	34	4.247
1994-95	2,122	24	203	20.994
1995-96	4,757	61	205	33.468
1996-97	8,598	118	408	59.520
1997-98	14,317	238	444	217.740
1998-99	32,995	571	2,633	558.935
1999-2000	1,14,775	1,930	7,715	1,958.237
2000-01	2,63,825	4,809	16,926	5,37.523
2001-02	4,61,478	10,263	27,539	10,463.598
2003-04	5,39,395	5454		

Source : NABARD Reports 2006.

In India, in 1992-93 there were only 255 SHGs, But in 2001-02, it rose to a great height of 4,61,478 SHGs. Here the time series equation found for India is Y = –172552 + 50624.3 X. X being the years considering 1992-93 as the first year.

In Tamilnadu, especially in South Tamilnadu this concept has become a very popular concept among the rural poor. In Tamilnadu, in 1992-93 there were 22 SHGs. From 1998-99, there is a steep rise. It rose to 2,633 SHGs. In 2001-02, it reached, 27,539 SHGs. Regression line of best fit for Tamilnadu is Y = –2376.0 + 796.082 X.

In Tamilnadu, introduction of Self Help Groups were in three different phases. In phase I Self Help Groups were started in the year 1997-98 but the micro-credit was introduced in January 1999. The first phase has covered the following districts, Vilupuram, Dharmapuri, Namakkal, Cuddalore, Ramnad, Thiruvarur, Vellore, Madurai, Thiruvalur, Salem, Karur, Thoothukudi, Theni and Virudhunagar.

In phase II, Self Help Groups were started in the year 1998-99 but the Micro-credit was given from January 1999 onwards. The second phase has covered the following districts. Sivagangai, Tirunelveli, Trichy, Thiruvannamalai, Pudukkottai, Nilgiris and Erode.

In phase III, Self Help Groups were started in the year 1999-2000. This phase covered Coimbatore, Kanchipuram, Kanyakumari, Perambalur, Thanjavur, Nagapattinam and Dindigul districts.

In Tamil Nadu Self Help Groups are growing at a faster rate. The Compound Growth Rate of Self Help Group in Tamilnadu is 124%, whereas the Growth Rate of Self Help Group in India is 119%. Self Help Groups are growing at a faster rate in South Tamil Nadu when compared to North Tamil Nadu.

Self Help Groups are the agencies which are very crucial in promoting thrift and finance mobilization. The existence of Self Help Groups helps empowering women and empowering the poor. Through these groups lot of public works and social works can be implemented.

To conclude, it was realised that Self Help Groups are still weak and are yet to train themselves in the field of micro-finance. It was also found out that this concept is popular among the women. Men also should be included. Advertising and marketing strategies need to be adopted. The Self Help Groups are working at different levels and from different experiences independently. The Self Help Groups are working as different islands and sometimes there is competition and difference of opinion among them. And hence networking will be a good solution. At present the Self Help Groups are shelters of illiterates and hence efforts can be made to attract the educated unemployed also. Through Marketing and canvassing mechanism, efforts should be made to attract more educated members.

Swami Vivekananda's words are very powerful and sure will make any reader to think about, 'I ask earnestly to open girls' schools in every village. If women are educated . . . culture, knowledge, power and devotion awaken in the land. That nation which does not respect women, has never become great, nor will ever in future . . . the principle reason why our race has so much degenerated is that we have no respect for these living images of Shakti'.

11

Constraints and Suggestions for Women Empowerment

In the process of development though women and their contribution towards science is growing, the growth remains incomparable with men. But still the gap continues to widens due to a lot of impediments on their way. The speed breakers of women developments are many. Some of the crucial issues are yet to be identified. Many issues are discussed in earlier chapters. Other than that the following are few of the important issues.

It starts with the historical impediments. Our cultural history and Political history has proved that women were considered as a secondary human being.

RELIGIOUS CONSTRAINTS

The birth of a son is bliss incarnate, while that of a daughter is the root of family misery. Only the sons are the heirs of their parents and they are eligible to do the final rites of their parents.[1] Almost all the religions project women inferior to men.

SOCIAL CONSTRAINTS

The serious social evils like sati, ill-treatment of widows and divorcees, ban on widow remarriage, dowry system, polygamy, child marriage, denial of property rights, denial of women education, temple prostitution, custom of purdah, abortion of girl babies, female infanticide, wife battering, bride burning, rape, abduction and sexual harassment are slowly reducing in India. But some of the problems still exist.

Indian social structure which constitutes religion, caste, custom, tradition, culture, family structure and other social institutions remind every one that woman is inferior.

NATURAL CONSTRAINTS

The physical make up, the strength and stamina differ from each other. Men need more calories to fulfil their physical requirement.

The naturality of child birth and child rearing makes women's life hectic. The psychological trauma and the physical pains undergone during the menstruation, menopause and child birth, etc. allows them to grow only at a very slow rate. The diseases associated in all these processes also add to the trauma. Pregnant Indian women have the world's highest levels of anaemia.[2]

Child psychology books say that girls mental I.Q.-level is high when compared to boys up to the age of 10 to 12. After 10 to 12 the boys' I.Q. exceeds girls' I.Q. This may be due to the natural impediments.

INFRASTRUCTURAL CONSTRAINTS

The pattern of education is also spoon feeding in the form of examinations, where there is less scope for overall personality development. Many of the rural schools could not provide water, toilet and such facilities for the girls. There is less awareness about the schemes, scholarships, financial incentives and programmes available for women.

PSYCHOLOGICAL CONSTRAINTS

The role conflict of the women also makes them psychologically inferior. Women have to play a dual role if they opt for career life. Priority cannot be given for any of these roles. And hence the psychological and emotional pressures lead to lots of trauma.

OTHER PROBLEMS

There are also some physical and mental injustices done to women which put them in a lower position in both organized and unorganized sectors.

1. Eve teasing.
2. Wife beating and wife battering.
3. Bigamy and Polygamy.
4. Rape and desertion.
5. Discrimination in male and female child especially in food.
6. No property rights for women in practice.
7. Social outlook against widow remarriage.
8. Unequal remuneration in manual jobs.
9. Dowry which leads to evils like.

    - Abortion of female foetus
    - Female infanticide
    - Child marriage
    - Dowry harassments leading to Dowry deaths.

The foremost problem among these is low self-development and low self-esteem. Lack of motivation and fear of failure and criticism suppress them in the society. The second reason may be the naturality of child birth, which makes them more responsible towards child rearing and household work. The third reason may be the social factor like caste, religion, customs and traditions. The dominating reason may be lack of awareness. To conclude, good social environment has to be enabled by the government to promote women to participate in various fields. More efforts should be taken to bring about good self-development among women even from their childhood days.

SUGGESTIONS

Several measures are taken to bring parity between both sexes, to bridge the gender gulf in all areas of development. In addition to that some more suggestions are given to augment the female human potential.

- *Self Development of Women*: Trainings, workshops and courses may be organised, so as to raise the self-esteem of the women, irrespective of their literacy.
- *Personality Development of Women*: The various dimensions of women personality has to be developed so that their confidence is raised to face any situation.
- Uniqueness of every gender has to be taught to women so as to make them accept the realities. The awareness of their uniqueness will be their weapon to defend themselves from various social evils.
- Women should have a separate curriculum for their development. They should not try to imitate men.
- *Focus on Women Role Models*: Women experts from academic or non-academic background should be projected as role models. The elite among the women also should come forward voluntarily to help the fellow women to come up. Professional jealousy and unhealthy competition among women should be discouraged.
- *Women Education*: Women education should be promoted and emphasised. So as to achieve this target and to reduce the women drop-outs, following efforts may be taken:
    - Girls schools and girls' colleges should be promoted.
    - In every schools and colleges, especially which are in rural area, toilet with proper facilities for ladies should be provided.
    - In lieu of the household responsibilities flexible timings may be fixed.

- ❖ For the security of girl students, ladies special buses should ply from all villages to various schools according to the school timings.

- *Pattern of Education*: The educational pattern followed should promote the women students originality. Overall personality development should be the target of education. Individual science projects and exhibitions should be made a part of curriculum
- *Training of Teachers*: All school and College teachers should be trained to be effective guides and counsellors. Emotional expressions of teachers and improper handling of students like beating will de-motivate them. And hence teachers should be trained by the government to be effective communicators.
- Women themselves should take few steps to elevate themselves in the society. They should be aware of their status and they should take risks visibility at work force. They should focus on continuous self-development. They should also be ready to market their skills.
- Compulsory education has to be accompanied by legislative and social action.
- *Provision of Services*: Services like crèches, door delivery of food, mobile health care, etc. should be promoted so as to enable women to be free to devote time to educate themselves to grow in their field of research.
- *Gender Sensitivity Camps*: Camps should be organised in backward and remote areas to develop the right attitude towards women.
- *Distance Education*: Extension education, and distance education should be promoted for women in a user friendly manner with a high scope for their overall development.
- *Economic Development*: The overall economic development of the country will help the women to prosper.
- *Improvement in Global Trade*: Oostendorp (2004) investigated the pact of trade liberalisation on the gender wage gap in 158 countries both developed and

developing. Regression analysis shows a negative relationship between trade integration (i.e. ratio of trade to G.D.P) and occupational wage gaps. And hence the labour market gender discrimination falls with increasing trade. And therefore increase in trade will reduce gender gap.

- Creating legal awareness among women and equipping them with the knowledge of their legal rights and with a capacity to use these rights.
- Assisting women in redressal of their grievances through Pre-litigation services.
- Facilitating speedy delivery of justice to women by organizing Lok Adalats in different parts of the country.
- Organizing promotional activities to mobilize women.
- Investigate and examine the existing provisions of the Constitution and all matters relating to the safeguards provided for women under the Constitution and other laws.
- Special studies, researches or investigations into specific problems or situations arising out of discrimination and atrocities against women.

Of late, Higher Education has become a global market commodity. Globalization or inter-nationalization of education will bring about a bright future for women.

In olden days when the male was the breadwinner of the family and woman was the homemaker, there was no question of bias. But of late, when women are educated and employed in economic activities, there arise the problems of ego boundaries of male and female and women's role conflict.

As a result, lot of debates are going on—most of them supporting women. Target of every family is love, friendship and happiness, not a war between male and female.

Constitutionally and legally women in India have equal status with women. Some special favours are also given for women.

1. 33% special reservation for women.

2. Reservation for women while contesting in Elections.
3. Special incentives for women entrepreneurs.
4. In private concerns women work less time for safety reasons and no night duties.
5. Divorce rules are hard towards men. They can not have the custody of children.
6. Special tax concessions for females.
7. Special ladies buses are plying.
8. Special ladies coaches are available in trains.
9. Special girl's schools, women colleges and women universities are existing.
10. In railways senior citizen concession for female is 50% and but for men it is 30% only.
11. Special gift of dowry in cash and jewels are given by parents to their girl children only.

Men and women play different roles in society with their gender differences shaped by biological, ideological, historical, religious, ethnic, economic and cultural determinants. To conclude each gender is unique. When one accepts his/her own uniqueness, his/her self-esteem goes up and he/she feels confident to face the society, in turn they will respect each other.

Notes and References

1. S.R.P. Bakshi and Kiran Bala, Social Status and Role of Women (Deep & Deep Publications).
2. India facts and Figures, page 19.

12

Protection of Women Rights in India

Indian government has taken special efforts to protect the suppressed women group. Fundamental Rights, among others, ensures equality before the law, equal protection of law, prohibits discrimination against any citizen on grounds of religion, race, caste, sex or place of birth, and guarantees equality of opportunity to all citizens in matters relating to employment through various articles like 14, 15, 15(3), 16, 39(a), 39(b), 39(c) and 42 of the constitution.

1. CONSTITUTIONAL PRIVILEGES

(i) Equality before law for women *(Article 14)*.

(ii) The State not to discriminate against any citizen on grounds only of religion, race, caste, sex, place of birth or any of them *(Article 15(i))*.

(iii) The State to make any special provision in favour of women and children *(Article 15 (3))*.

(iv) Equality of opportunity for all citizens in matters

relating to employment or appointment to any office under the state *(Article 16)*.

(v) The State to direct its policy towards securing for men and women equally the right to an adequate means of livelihood *(Article 39 (a))*; and equal pay for equal work for both men and women *(Article 39 (d))*.

(vi) To promote justice, on a basis of equal opportunity and to provide free legal aid by suitable legislation or scheme or in any other way to ensure that opportunities for securing justice are not denied to any citizen by reason of economic or other disabilities *(Article 39 A)*.

(vii) The State to make provision for securing just and humane conditions of work and for maternity relief *(Article 42)*.

(viii) The State to promote with special care the educational and economic interests of the weaker sections of the people and to protect them from social injustice and all forms of exploitation *(Article 46)*.

(ix) The State to raise the level of nutrition and the standard of living of its people and the improvement of public health *(Article 47)*.

(x) To promote harmony and the spirit of common brotherhood amongst all the people of India and to renounce practices derogatory to the dignity of women *(Article 51 (A) (e))*.

(xi) Not less than one-third (including the number of seats reserved for women belonging to the Scheduled Castes and the Scheduled Tribes) of the total number of seats to be filled by direct election in every Panchayat to be reserved for women and such seats to be allotted by rotation to different constituencies in a Panchayat *(Article 243 D (3))*.

(xii) Not less than one-third of the total number of offices of Chairpersons in the Panchayats at each level to be reserved for women *(Article 243 D (4))*.

(xiii) Not less than one-third (including the number of seats reserved for women belonging to the Scheduled Castes and the Scheduled Tribes) of the total number of seats to be filled by direct election in every Municipality to be reserved for women and such seats to be allotted by rotation to different constituencies in a Municipality *(Article 243 T(3))*

(xiv) Reservation of offices of Chairpersons in Municipalities for the Scheduled Castes, the Scheduled Tribes and women in such manner as the legislature of a State may by law provide *(Article 243 T (4))*.

2. LEGAL PROVISIONS

To uphold the Constitutional mandate, the State has enacted various legislative measures intended to ensure equal rights, to counter social discrimination and various forms of violence and atrocities and to provide support services especially to working women.

Although women may be victims of any of the crimes such as 'Murder', 'Robbery', 'Cheating', etc., the crimes, which are directed specifically against women, are characterized as 'Crime Against Women'. These are broadly classified under two categories.

1. The Crimes Identified Under the Indian Penal Code (IPC)

(i) Rape (Sec. 376 IPC)
(ii) Kidnapping & Abduction for different purposes (Secs. 363-373)
(iii) Homicide for Dowry, Dowry Deaths or their attempts (Secs. 302/304-B IPC)
(iv) Torture, both mental and physical (Sec. 498-A IPC)
(v) Molestation (Sec. 354 IPC)
(vi) Sexual Harassment (Sec. 509 IPC)
(vii) Importation of girls (upto 21 years of age)

2. The Crimes Identified under the Special Laws (SLL)

Although all laws are not gender specific, the provisions of law affecting women significantly have been reviewed periodically and amendments carried out to keep pace with the emerging requirements. Some acts which have special provisions to safeguard women and their interests are:

(i) The Employees State Insurance Act, 1948
(ii) The Plantation Labour Act, 1951
(iii) The Family Courts Act, 1954
(iv) The Special Marriage Act, 1954
(v) The Hindu Marriage Act, 1955
(vi) The Hindu Succession Act, 1986
(vii) Immoral Traffic (Prevention) Act, 1956
(viii) The Maternity Benefit Act, 1961 (Amended in 1995)
(ix) Dowry Prohibition Act, 1961
(x) The Medical Termination of Pregnacy Act, 1971
(xi) The Contract Labour (Regulation and Abolition) Act, 1976
(xii) The Equal Remuneration Act, 1976
(xiii) The Child Marriage Restraint (Amendment) Act, 1979
(xiv) The Criminal Law (Amendment) Act, 1983
(xv) The Factories (Amendment) Act, 1986
(xvi) Indecent Representation of Women (Prohibition) Act, 1986
(xvii) Commission of Sati (Prevention) Act, 1987

3. Special Initiatives for Women

(i) National Commission for Women

In January 1992, the Government set-up this statutory body with a specific mandate to study and monitor all matters relating to the constitutional and legal safeguards provided for women, review the existing legislation to suggest amendments wherever necessary, etc.

(ii) Reservation for Women in Local Self-Government

The 72nd and 73rd Constitutional Amendment Acts passed in 1992 by Parliament ensure one-third of the total seats for women in all elected offices in local bodies whether in rural areas or urban areas.

(iii) The National Plan of Action for Girl Child (1991-2000)

The Plan of Action is to ensure survival, protection and development of the girl child with the ultimate objective of building up a better future for the girl child.

(iv) National Policy for the Empowerment of Women, 2001

The Department of Women and Child Development in the Ministry of Human Resource Development has prepared a *"National Policy for the Empowerment of Women"* in the year 2001. The goal of this policy is to bring about the advancement, development and empowerment of women.

The goal of the National Policy for the empowerment of women is to bring about the advancement, development and empowerment of women. Some of the specific objectives of this policy are: (a) Creating an environment through positive economic and social policies for full development of women to enable them to realize their full potential, (b) Equal access to health care, quality education at all levels, career and vocational guidance, etc., (c) Elimination of discrimination and all forms of violence against women and girl child.

The policy also provides for economic empowerment through poverty eradication, micro credit programmes, training of women to facilitate them in playing efficient role in agriculture and industry. The social empowerment of women is facilitated through effective provisions of Education, Health, Nutrition, Drinking water and Sanitation, gender sensitization, etc. Elimination of all forms of violence against women, physical and mental, whether at domestic or societal levels, including those arising from customs, traditions and accepted practices. A *National Resource Center for Women (NRCW)* is being set-up which will provide relevant technical back up for the successful implementation of the policy.

The Government has also committed the following provisions to ensure women's rights and women empowerment. Some of the commitments are:

1. The principle of gender equality is enshrined in the Indian Constitution in its Preamble, Fundamental Rights, Fundamental Duties and Directive Principles. The Constitution not only grants equality to women, but also empowers the State to adopt measures of positive discrimination in favour of women.
2. Within the framework of a democratic polity, our laws, development policies, Plans and programmes have

aimed at women's advancement in different spheres. From the Fifth Five Year Plan (1974-78) onwards has been a marked shift in the approach to women's issues from welfare to development. In recent years, the empowerment of women has been recognized as the central issue in determining the status of women. The National Commission for Women was set-up by an Act of Parliament in 1990 to safeguard the rights and legal entitlements of women. The 73rd and 74th Amendments (1993) to the Constitution of India have provided for reservation of seats in the local bodies of Panchayats and Municipalities for women, laying a strong foundation for their participation in decision-making at the local levels.

3. India has also ratified various international conventions and human rights instruments committing to secure equal rights of women. Key among them is the ratification of the Convention on Elimination of All Forms of Discrimination Against Women (CEDAW) in 1993.
4. The Mexico Plan of Action (1975), the Nairobi Forward Looking Strategies (1985), the Beijing Declaration as well as the Platform for Action (1995) and the Outcome Document adopted by the UNGA Session on Gender Equality and Development and Peace for the 21st century, titled "Further actions and initiatives to implement the Beijing Declaration and the Platform for Action" have been unreservedly endorsed by India for appropriate follow-up.
5. The Policy also takes note of the commitments of the Ninth Five Year Plan and the other Sectoral Policies relating to empowerment of Women.
6. The women's movement and a wide-spread network of non-Government Organisations which have strong grass-roots presence and deep insight into women's concerns have contributed in inspiring initiatives for the empowerment of women.
7. However, there still exists a wide gap between the goals enunciated in the Constitution, legislation, policies, plans, programmes, and related mechanisms

on the one hand and the situational reality of the status of women in India, on the other. This has been analyzed extensively in the Report of the Committee on the Status of Women in India, "Towards Equality", 1974 and highlighted in the National Perspective Plan for Women, 1988-2000, the Shramshakti Report, 1988 and the Platform for Action, Five Years After—An assessment".

8. Gender disparity manifests itself in various forms, the most obvious being the trend of continuously declining female ratio in the population in the last few decades. Social stereotyping and violence at the domestic and societal levels are some of the other manifestations. Discrimination against girl children, adolescent girls and women persists in parts of the country.
9. The underlying causes of gender inequality are related to social and economic structure, which is based on informal and formal norms and practices.
10. Consequently, the access of women particularly those belonging to weaker sections including Scheduled Castes/Scheduled Tribes/Other Backward Classes and minorities, majority of whom are in the rural areas and in the informal, unorganized sector—to education, health and productive resources, among others, is inadequate. Therefore, they remain largely marginalized, poor and socially excluded.

(v) Mainstreaming a Gender Perspective in the Development Process

1. Policies, programmes and systems will be established to ensure mainstreaming of women's perspectives in all developmental processes, as catalysts, participants and recipients. Wherever there are gaps in policies and programmes, women specific interventions would be undertaken to bridge these. Coordinating and monitoring mechanisms will also be devised to assess from time to time the progress of such mainstreaming mechanisms. Women's issues and concerns as a result will specially be addressed and reflected in all concerned laws, sectoral policies, plans and programmes of action.

(vi) Economic Empowerment of Women

1. Poverty Eradication

Since women comprise the majority of the population below the poverty line and are very often in situations of extreme poverty, given the harsh realities of intra-household and social discrimination, macro-economic policies and poverty eradication programmes will specifically address the needs and problems of such women. There will be improved implementation of programmes which are already women-oriented with special targets for women. Steps will be taken for mobilization of poor women and convergence of services, by offering them a range of economic and social options, along with necessary support measures to enhance their capabilities.

2. Micro Credit

In order to enhance women's access to credit for consumption and production, the establishment of new, and strengthening of existing micro-credit mechanisms and micro-finance institution will be undertaken so that the outreach of credit is enhanced. Other supportive measures would be taken to ensure adequate flow of credit through extant financial institutions and banks, so that all women below poverty line have easy access to credit.

3. Women and Economy

Women's perspectives will be included in designing and implementing macro-economic and social policies by institutionalizing their participation in such processes. Their contribution to socio-economic development as producers and workers will be recognized in the formal and informal sectors (including home-based workers) and appropriate policies relating to employment and to her working conditions will be drawn up. Such measures could include:

(a) Reinterpretation and redefinition of conventional concepts of work wherever necessary, e.g. in the Census records, to reflect women's contribution as producers and workers.

(b) Preparation of satellite and national accounts.

(c) Development of appropriate methodologies for undertaking (i) and (ii) above.

4. *Globalization*

Globalization has presented new challenges for the realization of the goal of women's equality, the gender impact of which has not been systematically evaluated fully. However, from the micro-level studies that were commissioned by the Department of Women and Child Development, it is evident that there is a need for re-framing policies for access to employment and quality of employment. Benefits of the growing global economy have been unevenly distributed leading to wider economic disparities, the feminization of poverty, increased gender inequality through often deteriorating working conditions and unsafe working environment especially in the informal economy and rural areas. Strategies will be designed to enhance the capacity of women and empower them to meet the negative social and economic impacts, which may flow from the globalization process.

5. *Women and Agriculture*

In view of the critical role of women in the agriculture and allied sectors, as producers, concentrated efforts will be made to ensure that benefits of training, extension and various programmes will reach them in proportion to their numbers. The programmes for training women in soil conservation, social forestry, dairy development and other occupations allied to agriculture like horticulture, livestock including small animal husbandry, poultry, fisheries, etc. will be expanded to benefit women workers in the agriculture sector.

6. *Women and Industry*

The important role played by women in electronics, information technology and food processing and agro-industry and textiles has been crucial to the development of these sectors. They would be given comprehensive support in terms of labour legislation, social security and other support services to participate in various industrial sectors.

Women at present cannot work in night shift in factories even if they wish to. Suitable measures will be taken to enable women to work on the night shift in factories. This will be accompanied with support services for security, transportation etc.

7. Support Services

The provision of support services for women, like child care facilities, including crèches at work places and educational institutions, homes for the aged and the disabled will be expanded and improved to create an enabling environment and to ensure their full cooperation in social, political and economic life. Women-friendly personnel policies will also be drawn up to encourage women to participate effectively in the developmental process.

(vii) Social Empowerment of Women

1. Education

Equal access to education for women and girls will be ensured. Special measures will be taken to eliminate discrimination, universalize education, eradicate illiteracy, create a gender-sensitive educational system, increase enrolment and retention rates of girls and improve the quality of education to facilitate life-long learning as well as development of occupation/vocation/technical skills by women. Reducing the gender gap in secondary and higher education would be a focus area. Sectoral time targets in existing policies will be achieved, with a special focus on girls and women, particularly those belonging to weaker sections including the Scheduled Castes/ Scheduled Tribes/Other Backward Classes/Minorities. Gender sensitive curricula would be developed at all levels of educational system in order to address sex stereotyping as one of the causes of gender discrimination.

2. Health

A holistic approach to women's health which includes both nutrition and health services will be adopted and special attention will be given to the needs of women and the girl at all stages of the life cycle. The reduction of infant mortality and maternal mortality, which are sensitive indicators of human development, is a priority concern. This policy reiterates the national demographic goals for Infant Mortality Rate (IMR), Maternal Mortality Rate (MMR) set out in the National Population Policy, 2000. Women should have access to comprehensive, affordable and quality health care. Measures will be adopted that take into account the reproductive rights of women to enable them to exercise informed choices, their vulnerability to sexual and health problems together with endemic, infectious and communicable diseases such as malaria, TB, and water borne diseases as well as hypertension and cardio-pulmonary diseases. The social, developmental and health consequences of HIV/AIDS and other sexually transmitted diseases will be tackled from a gender perspective.

To effectively meet problems of infant and maternal mortality, and early marriage the availability of good and accurate data at micro level on deaths, birth and marriages is required. Strict implementation of registration of births and deaths would be ensured and registration of marriages would be made compulsory.

In accordance with the commitment of the National Population Policy (2000) to population stabilization, this Policy recognizes the critical need of men and women to have access to safe, effective and affordable methods of family planning of their choice and the need to suitably address the issues of early marriages and spacing of children. Interventions such as spread of education, compulsory registration of marriage and special programmes like BSY should impact on delaying the age of marriage so that by 2010 child marriages are eliminated.

Women's traditional knowledge about health care and nutrition will be recognized through proper documentation and its use will be encouraged. The use of Indian and alternative systems of medicine will be enhanced within the framework of overall health infrastructure available for women.

3. *Nutrition*

In view of the high risk of malnutrition and disease that women face at all the three critical stages viz., infancy and childhood, adolescent and reproductive phase, focussed attention would be paid to meeting the nutritional needs of women at all stages of the life cycle. This is also important in view of the critical link between the health of adolescent girls, pregnant and lactating women with the health of infant and young children. Special efforts will be made to tackle the problem of macro and micro-nutrient deficiencies especially amongst pregnant and lactating women as it leads to various diseases and disabilities.

Intra-household discrimination in nutritional matters *vis-à-vis* girls and women will be sought to be ended through appropriate strategies. Widespread use of nutrition education would be made to address the issues of intra-household imbalances in nutrition and the special needs of pregnant and lactating women. Women's participation will also be ensured in the planning, superintendence and delivery of the system.

8. Drinking Water and Sanitation

Special attention will be given to the needs of women in the provision of safe drinking water, sewage disposal, toilet facilities and sanitation within accessible reach of households, especially in rural areas and urban slums. Women's participation will be ensured in the planning, delivery and maintenance of such services.

9. Housing and Shelter

Women's perspectives will be included in housing policies, planning of housing colonies and provision of shelter both in rural and urban areas. Special attention will be given for providing adequate and safe housing and accommodation for women including single women, heads of households, working women, students, apprentices and trainees.

10. Environment

Women will be involved and their perspectives reflected in the policies and programmes for environment, conservation and restoration. Considering the impact of environmental factors on their livelihoods, women's participation will be ensured in the conservation of the environment and control of environmental degradation. The vast majority of rural women still depend on the locally available non-commercial sources of energy such as animal dung, crop waste and fuel wood. In order to ensure the efficient use of these energy resources in an environmental friendly manner, the Policy will aim at promoting the programmes of non-conventional energy resources. Women will be involved in spreading the use of solar energy, biogas, smokeless chulahs and other rural application so as to have a visible impact of these measures in influencing eco system and in changing the life styles of rural women.

11. *Science and Technology*

Programmes will be strengthened to bring about a greater involvement of women in science and technology. These will include measures to motivate girls to take up science and technology for higher education and also ensure that development projects with scientific and technical inputs involve women fully. Efforts to develop a scientific temper and awareness will also be stepped up. Special measures would be taken for their training in areas where they have special skills like communication and information technology. Efforts to develop appropriate technologies suited to women's needs as well as to reduce their drudgery will be given a special focus too.

12. *Women in Difficult Circumstances*

In recognition of the diversity of women's situations and in acknowledgement of the needs of specially disadvantaged groups, measures and programmes will be undertaken to provide them with special assistance. These groups include women in extreme poverty, destitute women, women in conflict situations, women affected by natural calamities, women in less developed regions, the disabled widows, elderly women, single women in difficult circumstances, women heading households, those displaced from employment, migrants, women who are victims of marital violence, deserted women and prostitutes, etc.

(viii) Violence Against Women

All forms of violence against women, physical and mental, whether at domestic or societal levels, including those arising from customs, traditions or accepted practices shall be dealt with effectively with a view to eliminate its incidence. Institutions and mechanisms/schemes for assistance will be created and strengthened for prevention of such violence , including sexual harassment at work place and customs like dowry; for the rehabilitation of the victims of violence and for taking effective action against the perpetrators of such violence. A special emphasis will also be laid on programmes and measures to deal with trafficking in women and girls.

(ix) Rights of the Girl Child

All forms of discrimination against the girl child and violation of her rights shall be eliminated by undertaking strong measures both preventive and punitive within and outside the family. These would relate specifically to strict enforcement of laws against prenatal sex selection and the practices of female foeticide, female infanticide, child marriage, child abuse and child prostitution, etc. Removal of discrimination in the treatment of the girl child within the family and outside and projection of a positive image of the girl child will be actively fostered. There will be special emphasis on the needs of the girl child and earmarking of substantial investments in the areas relating to food and nutrition, health and education, and in vocational education. In implementing programmes for eliminating child labour, there will be a special focus on girl children.

(x) Mass Media

Media will be used to portray images consistent with human dignity of girls and women. The Policy will specifically strive to remove demeaning, degrading and negative conventional stereotypical images of women and violence against women. Private sector partners and media networks will be involved at all levels to ensure equal access for women particularly in the area of information and communication technologies. The media would be encouraged to develop codes of conduct, professional guidelines and other self-regulatory mechanisms to remove gender stereotypes and promote balanced portrayals of women and men.

(xi) Institutional Mechanisms

1. Institutional mechanisms, to promote the advancement of women, which exist at the Central and State levels, will be strengthened. These will be through interventions as may be appropriate and will relate to, among others, provision of adequate resources, training and advocacy skills to effectively influence macro-policies, legislation, programmes, etc. to achieve the empowerment of women.
2. National and State Councils will be formed to oversee the operationalisation of the Policy on a regular basis. The National Council will be headed by the Prime Minister and the State Councils by the Chief Ministers and be broad in composition having representatives from the concerned Departments/Ministries, National and State Commissions for Women, Social Welfare Boards, representatives of Non-Government Organizations, Women's Organisations, Corporate Sector, Trade Unions, financing institutions, academics, experts and social activists, etc. These bodies will review the progress made in implementing the Policy twice a year. The National Development Council will also be informed of the progress of the programme undertaken under the policy from time to time for advice and comments.
3. National and State Resource Centres on women will be established with mandates for collection and dissemination of information, undertaking research work, conducting surveys, implementing training and awareness generation programmes, etc. These Centers will link up with Women's Studies Centres and other research and academic institutions through suitable information networking systems.
4. While institutions at the district level will be strengthened, at the grass-roots, women will be helped by Government through its programmes to organize and strengthen into Self-Help Groups (SHGs) at the Anganwadi/Village/Town level. The women's groups will be helped to institutionalize themselves into registered societies and to federate at the Panchayat/

Municipal level. These societies will bring about synergistic implementation of all the social and economic development programmes by drawing resources made available through Government and Non-Government channels, including banks and financial institutions and by establishing a close Interface with the Panchayats/Municipalities.

(xii) Legislation

1. The existing legislative structure will be reviewed and additional legislative measures taken by identified departments to implement the Policy. This will also involve a review of all existing laws including personal, customary and tribal laws, subordinate legislation, related rules as well as executive and administrative regulations to eliminate all gender discriminatory references. The process will be planned over a time period 2000-03. The specific measures required would be evolved through a consultation process involving civil society, National Commission for Women and Department of Women and Child Development. In appropriate cases the consultation process would be widened to include other stakeholders too.
2. Effective implementation of legislation would be promoted by involving civil society and community. Appropriate changes in legislation will be undertaken, if necessary.
3. In addition, following other specific measures will be taken to implement the legislation effectively.

    (a) Strict enforcement of all relevant legal provisions and speedy redressal of grievances will be ensured, with a special focus on violence and gender related atrocities.

    (b) Measures to prevent and punish sexual harassment at the place of work, protection for women workers in the organized/unorganized sector and strict enforcement of relevant laws such as Equal Remuneration Act and Minimum Wages Act will be undertaken.

(c) Crimes against women, their incidence, prevention, investigation, detection and prosecution will be regularly reviewed at all Crime Review fora and Conferences at the Central, State and District levels. Recognised, local, voluntary organizations will be authorized to lodge complaints and facilitate registration, investigations and legal proceedings related to violence and atrocities against girls and women.

(d) Women's Cells in Police Stations, Encourage Women Police Stations Family Courts, Mahila Courts, Counselling Centers, Legal Aid Centers and Nyaya Panchayats will be strengthened and expanded to eliminate violence and atrocities against women.

(e) Widespread dissemination of information on all aspects of legal rights, human rights and other entitlements of women, through specially designed legal literacy programmes and rights information programmes will be done.

(xiii) Gender Sensitization

Training of personnel of executive, legislative and judicial wings of the State, with a special focus on policy and programme framers, implementation and development agencies, law enforcement machinery and the judiciary, as well as non-governmental organizations will be undertaken. Other measures will include:

(a) Promoting societal awareness to gender issues and women's human rights

(b) Review of curriculum and educational materials to include gender education and human rights issues.

(c) Removal of all references derogatory to the dignity of women from all public documents and legal instruments.

(d) Use of different forms of mass media to communicate social messages relating to women's equality and empowerment.

(xiv) Panchayati Raj Institutions

The 73rd and 74th Amendments (1993) to the Indian Constitution have served as a breakthrough towards ensuring equal access and increased participation in political power structure for women. The PRIs will play a central role in the process of enhancing women's participation in public life. The PRIs and the local self-Governments will be actively involved in the implementation and execution of the National Policy for Women at the grassroots level.

(xv) Partnership with the Voluntary Sector Organizations

The involvement of voluntary organizations, associations, federations, trade unions, non-governmental organizations, women's organizations, as well as institutions dealing with education, training and research will be ensured in the formulation, implementation, monitoring and review of all policies and programmes affecting women. Towards this end, they will be provided with appropriate support related to resources and capacity building and facilitated to participate actively in the process of the empowerment of women.

(xvi) International Cooperation

The Policy will aim at implementation of international obligations/commitments in all sectors on empowerment of women such as the Convention on All Forms of Discrimination Against Women (CEDAW), Convention on the Rights of the Child (CRC), International Conference on Population and Development (ICPD+5) and other such instruments. International, regional and sub-regional cooperation towards the empowerment of women will continue to be encouraged through sharing of experiences, exchange of ideas and technology, networking with institutions and organizations and through bilateral and multi-lateral partnerships.

13

The Protection of Women from Domestic Violence Act[1], 2005

(No. 43 of 2005 [13th September, 2005)

Today Indian Families are witnessing increased rate of matrimonial disputes and women are more vulnerable and they are often the passive victims of *Domestic Violence* in which they are harshly treated after marriage and in order to protect women from this and prevent the recurring occurrences of domestic violence, an Act called Domestic Violence Act 2005 was enacted by the parliament.

In general, the term "domestic violence" refers to violence that occurs in the home. Although violence in the home can be directed toward children, the elderly, or other household members, most often this term is used to represent violence between adolescents and/or adults especially husband and wife. And this act focus on this violence between adolescents and/or adults.

The *Protection of Women from Domestic Violence Act 2005* was brought into force by the Indian government from October 26, 2006. The Act was passed by the Parliament in August 2005 and assented to by the President on 13th September, 2005. As of November 2007, it has been ratified by four of twenty-eight state governments in India; namely Andhra Pradesh, Tamil Nadu, Uttar Pradesh and Orissa. Of about 8,000 criminal cases registered all over India under this act.

DEFINITION

DOMESTIC VIOLENCE (1) For the purposes of this Act, any conduct of the respondent shall constitute domestic violence if he—(a) habitually assaults or makes the life of the aggrieved person miserable by cruelty of conduct even if such conduct does not amount to physical ill-treatment; or (b) forces the aggrieved person to lead an immoral life; or (c) otherwise injures or harms the aggrieved person. (2) Nothing contained in clause (c) of sub-section (1) shall amount to domestic violence if the pursuit of course of conduct by the respondent was reasonable for his own protection or for the protection of his or another's property.

The Act has also defined Physical Violence very comprehensively, as:

- Any kind of bodily harm or injury.
- A threat of bodily harm.
- Beating, slapping and hitting.

Thus, physical violence is defined as any act or conduct which is of such a nature as to cause bodily pain, harm, or danger to life, limb, or health, or an act that impairs the health or development of the person aggrieved, or that includes assault, criminal intimidation and criminal force.

But violence against women is not always physical. For the first time, the law has expanded the definition to include sexual, verbal and economic violence.

Under the law, Sexual Violence will include:

- Forced sexual encounter
- Forcing a woman to look at pornography or any obscene pictures
- Any act of sexual nature to abuse, humiliate or degrade a woman's' integrity.

The new law is also tough on men who subject women to name calling or verbal abuse. While Verbal Violence is often trivialized as unimportant, observers say it can damage a woman's self-esteem

The Act defines Verbal Violence as:

- Name calling.
- Any kind of accusation on a woman's character or conduct.
- Insults for not bringing dowry.
- Preventing a woman from marrying a person of her choice.
- Any form of threat or insults for not producing a male child.

Another significant step has been to recognize Economic Violence. Under the Act, Economic Violence is:

- Not providing money, food, clothes, medicines
- Causing hindrance to employment opportunities
- Forcing a woman to vacate her house
- Not paying rent.

This provision comes into play in instances of marital disputes, where the husband tends to deprive the wife of necessary money as a weapon. The law also sees a husband who sells off his wife's jewellery and assets as being guilty of economic abuse.

SALIENT FEATURES OF THE ACT

It is a comprehensive law and addresses all issues related to women. It is for the first time that an act has been made to address women's issues in such detail. The Act is an extremely progressive one not only because it recognizes women who are in a live in relationship but also extends protection to other women in the household, including sisters and mothers thus the Act includes relations of consanguinity, marriage, or through relationships in the nature of marriage, adoption, or joint family thus, 'domestic relationships' are not restricted to the marital context alone.

- Harassment by way of unlawful dowry demands to the woman or her relatives would also be covered under this definition.
- Husbands or live-in partners who would be guilty of domestic violence can be put behind bars for a year and fined Rs. 20,000
- And all crimes in the Domestic Violence Act are non-bailable.
- The Act seeks to cover those women who are or have been in a relationship with the abuser where both parties have lived together in a shared household and are related by consanguinity, marriage or a relationship in the nature of marriage, or adoption; in addition relationship with family members living together as a joint family are also included. Even those women who are sisters, widows, mothers, single women, or living with the abuser are entitled to get legal protection under the proposed Act.
- "Domestic violence" includes actual abuse or the threat of abuse that is physical, sexual, verbal, emotional and economic. Harassment by way of unlawful dowry demands to the woman or her relatives would also be covered under this definition.
- One of the most important features of the Act is the woman's right to secure housing. The Act provides for the woman's right to reside in the matrimonial or shared household, whether or not she has any title or rights in the household. This right is secured by a residence order, which is passed by a court. These residence orders cannot be passed against anyone who is a woman.
- The other relief envisaged under the Act is that of the power of the court to pass protection orders that prevent the abuser from aiding or committing an act of domestic violence or any other specified act, entering a workplace or any other place frequented by the abused, attempting to communicate with the abused, isolating any assets used by both the parties and causing violence to the abused, her relatives and others who provide her assistance from the domestic violence.

- The draft Act provides for appointment of Protection Officers and NGOs to provide assistance to the woman w.r.t medical examination, legal aid, safe shelter, etc.
- The Act provides for breach of protection order or interim protection order by the respondent as a cognizable and non-bailable offence punishable with imprisonment for a term which may extend to one year or with fine which may extend to twenty thousand rupees or with both. Similarly, non-compliance or discharge of duties by the Protection Officer is also sought to be made an offence under the Act with similar punishment.
- A women who is the victim of domestic violence will have the right to the services of the police, shelter homes and medical establishments. She also has the right to simultaneously file her own complaint under Section 498A of the Indian Penal Code.
- Sections 18-23 of the Act provide a large number of avenues for an abused women to get relief. She can get through the courts. Protection Orders, Residence Orders, Monetary Relief, Custody Order for her children, Compensation Order and Interim/*Ex parte* Orders.

The other relief envisaged under the Act is that of the power of the court to pass protection orders that prevent the abuser from aiding or committing an act of domestic violence or any other specified act, entering a workplace or any other place frequented by the abused, attempting to communicate with the abused, isolating any assets used by both the parties and causing violence to the abused, her relatives and others who provide her assistance from the domestic violence.

FEW PROVISION FROM THE ACT

Section 1 (Chapter 1) : PRELIMINARY

An Act to provide for more effective protection of the rights of women guaranteed under the Constitution who are victims of violence of any kind occurring within the family and for matters connected therewith or incidental thereto. BE it enacted by Parliament in the Fifty-sixth Year of the Republic of India as follows:

(2) It extends to the whole of India except the State of Jammu and Kashmir.

(3) It shall come into force on such date as the Central Government may, by notification in the Official Gazette, appoint.

2. *Definition of concepts:* (a) *"aggrieved person"* means any woman who is, or has been, in a domestic relationship with the respondent and who alleges to have been subjected to any act of domestic violence by the respondent;

(e) *"domestic incident report"* means a report made in the prescribed form on receipt of a complaint of domestic violence from an aggrieved person;

(f) *"domestic relationship"* means a relationship between two persons who live or have, at any point of time, lived together in a shared household, when they are related by consanguinity, marriage, or through a relationship in the nature of marriage, adoption or are family members living together as a joint family;

Section 5 (Chapter 5) Definition of Domestic Violence

3. *Definition of domestic violence.* For the purposes of this Act, any act, omission or commission or conduct of the respondent shall constitute *domestic violence* in case it :

(a) *harms or injures or endangers the health, safety, life, limb or well-being, whether mental or physical, of the aggrieved person or tends to do so and includes causing physical abuse, sexual abuse, verbal and emotional abuse and economic abuse; or*

(b) *harasses, harms, injures or endangers the aggrieved person with a view to coerce her or any other person related to her to meet any unlawful demand for any dowry or other property or valuable security; or*

(c) *has the effect of threatening the aggrieved person or any person related to her by any conduct mentioned in clause (a) or clause (b); or (d) otherwise injures or causes harm, whether physical or mental, to the aggrieved person.*

Explanation I.—For the purposes of this section:

(i) *"physical abuse"* means any act or conduct which is of such a nature as to cause bodily pain, harm, or danger to life, limb, or health or impair the health or development of the aggrieved person and includes assault, criminal intimidation and criminal force;

(ii) *"sexual abuse"* includes any conduct of a sexual nature that abuses, humiliates, degrades or otherwise violates the dignity of woman;

(iii) *"verbal and emotional abuse"* includes—

(a) *insults, ridicule, humiliation, name calling and insults* or ridicule specially with regard to not having a child or a male child; and

(b) repeated *threats to cause physical pain* to any person in whom the aggrieved person is interested.

(iv) *"economic abuse"* includes—

(a) *deprivation of all or any economic or financial resources* to which the aggrieved person is entitled under any law or custom whether payable under an order of a court or otherwise or which the aggrieved person requires out of necessity including, but not limited to, household necessities for the aggrieved person and her children, if any, stridhan, property, jointly or separately owned by the aggrieved person, payment of rental related to the shared household and maintenance;

(b) *disposal of household effects,* any alienation of assets whether movable or immovable, valuables, shares, securities, bonds and the like or other property in which the aggrieved person has an interest or is entitled to use by virtue of the domestic relationship or which may be reasonably required by the aggrieved person or her children or her stridhan or any other property jointly or separately held by the aggrieved person; and

(c) *prohibition or restriction to continued access to resources or facilities* which the aggrieved person is entitled to use or enjoy by virtue of the domestic relationship including access to the shared household.

Explanation II.—For the purpose of determining whether any act, omission, commission or conduct of the respondent constitutes "domestic violence" under this section, the overall facts and circumstances of the case shall be taken into consideration.

Section 7 (Chapter 7) Information to Protection Officer and exclusion of liability of informant.

4. Information to Protection Officer and exclusion of liability of informant—(1)Any person who has reason to believe that an act of domestic violence has been, or is being, or is likely to be committed, may give information about it to the concerned Protection Officer.

(2) No liability, civil or criminal, shall be incurred by any person for giving in good faith of information for the purpose of sub-section (1).

Duties of police officers, service providers and Magistrate—A police officer, Protection Officer, service provider or Magistrate who has received a complaint of domestic violence or is otherwise present at the place of an incident of domestic violence or when the incident of domestic violence is reported to him, shall inform the aggrieved person-(a) of her right to make an application for obtaining a relief by way of a protection order, an order for monetary relief, a custody order, a residence order, a compensation order or more than one such order under this Act;(b) of the availability of services of service providers;(c) of the availability of services of the Protection Officers;(d) of her right to free legal services under the *Legal Services Authorities Act, 1987 (39 of 1987)*;(e) of her right to file a complaint under section[2] S498A of the Indian Penal Code[3] 45 of 1860 (45 of 1860), wherever relevant: Provided that nothing in this Act shall be construed in any manner as to relieve a police officer from his duty to proceed in accordance with law upon receipt of information as to the commission of a cognizable offence.

Section 9 (Chapter 9) : Duties of Shelter Homes

6. *Duties of shelter homes* : If an aggrieved person or on her behalf a *Protection Officer* or a service provider requests the person in charge of a shelter home to provide shelter to her, such person in charge of the shelter home shall provide shelter to the aggrieved person in the shelter home.

Section 10 (Chapter 10) : Duties of Medical Facilities

7. *Duties of medical facilities* : If an aggrieved person or, on her behalf a Protection Officer or a service provider requests the person in charge of a medical facility to provide any medical aid to her, such person in charge of the medical facility shall provide medical aid to the aggrieved person in the medical facility.

Section 11 (Chapter 11) : Appointment of Protection Officers

8. *Appointment of Protection Officers* : (1) The State Government shall, by notification, appoint such number of *Protection Officers* in each district as it may consider necessary and shall also notify the area or areas within which a Protection Officer shall exercise the powers and perform the duties conferred on him by or under this Act.

(2) The *Protection Officers* shall as far as possible be women and shall possess such qualifications and experience as may be prescribed.

(3) The terms and conditions of service of the *Protection Officer* and the other officers subordinate to him shall be such as may be prescribed.

Section 12 (Chapter 12) : Duties and Functions of Protection Officers

9. *Duties and functions of Protection Officers* : (1) It shall be the duty of the Protection Officer—

(a) to assist the Magistrate in the discharge of his functions under this Act;

(b) to make a domestic incident report to the Magistrate, in such form and in such manner as may be prescribed, upon receipt of a complaint of domestic violence and forward copies thereof to the police officer in charge of the police station within the local limits of whose jurisdiction domestic violence is alleged to have been committed and to the service providers in that area;

(c) to make an application in such form and in such manner as may be prescribed to the Magistrate, if the aggrieved person so desires, claiming relief for issuance of a protection order;

(d) to ensure that the aggrieved person is provided legal aid under the Legal Services Authorities Act, 1987 (39 of 1987) and make available free of cost the prescribed form in which a complaint is to be made;

(e) to maintain a list of all service providers providing legal aid or counselling, shelter homes and medical facilities in a local area within the jurisdiction of the Magistrate;

(f) to make available a safe shelter home, if the aggrieved person so requires and forward a copy of his report of having lodged the aggrieved person in a shelter home to the police station and the Magistrate having jurisdiction in the area where the shelter home is situated;

(g) to get the aggrieved person medically examined, if she has sustained bodily injuries and forward a copy of the medical report to the police station and the Magistrate having jurisdiction in the area where the domestic violence is alleged to have been taken place;

(h) to ensure that the order for monetary relief under section 20 is complied with and executed, in accordance with the procedure prescribed under the *Code of Criminal Procedure, 1973* (2 of 1974); and (i) to perform such other duties as may be prescribed.

(2) The Protection Officer shall be under the control and supervision of the Magistrate, and shall perform the duties imposed on him by the Magistrate and the Government by, or under, this Act..

Section 13 (Chapter 13) : Service Providers

10. Service providers.—(1) Subject to such rules as may be made in this behalf, any voluntary association registered under

the Societies Registration Act, 1860 (21 of 1860) or a company registered under the Companies Act, 1956 (1 of 1956) or any other law for the time being in force with the objective of protecting the rights and interests of women by any lawful means including providing of legal aid, medical, financial or other assistance shall register itself with the State Government as a service provider for the purposes of this Act.

(2) A service provider registered under sub-section (1) shall have the power to:

(a) record the domestic incident report in the prescribed form if the aggrieved person so desires and forward a copy thereof to the Magistrate and the Protection Officer having jurisdiction in the area where the domestic violence took place;
(b) get the aggrieved person medically examined and forward a copy of the medical report to the Protection Officer and the police station within the local limits of which the domestic violence took place;
(c) ensure that the aggrieved person is provided shelter in a shelter home, if she so requires and forward a report of the lodging of the aggrieved person in the shelter home to the police station within the local limits of which the domestic violence took place.

(3) No suit, prosecution or other legal proceeding shall lie against any service provider or any member of the service provider who is, or who is deemed to be, acting or purporting to act under this Act, for anything which is in good faith done or intended to be done in the exercise of powers or discharge of functions under this Act towards the prevention of the commission of domestic violence.

Section 14 (Chapter 14) : Duties of Government

11. *Duties of Government.*—The Central Government and every State Government, shall take all measures to ensure that:

(a) the provisions of this Act are given wide publicity through public media including the television, radio and the print media at regular intervals;

(b) the Central Government and State Government officers including the police officers and the members of the judicial services are given periodic sensitization and awareness training on the issues addressed by this Act;
(c) effective co-ordination between the services provided by concerned Ministries and Departments dealing with law, home affairs including law and order, health and human resources to address issues of domestic violence is established and periodical review of the same is conducted; and
(d) protocols for the various Ministries concerned with the delivery of services to women under this Act including the courts are prepared and put in place.

Section 16 (Chapter 16) : Application to Magistrate

12. *Application to Magistrate.*—(1) An aggrieved person or a Protection Officer or any other person on behalf of the aggrieved person may present an application to the Magistrate seeking one or more reliefs under this Act:

Provided that before passing any order on such application, the Magistrate shall take into consideration any domestic incident report received by him from the Protection Officer or the service provider.

(2) The relief sought for under sub-section (1) may include a relief for issuance of an order for payment of compensation or damages without prejudice to the right of such person to institute a suit for compensation or damages for the injuries caused by the acts of domestic violence committed by the respondent: Provided that where a decree for any amount as compensation or damages has been passed by any court in favour of the aggrieved person, the amount, if any, paid or payable in pursuance of the order made by the Magistrate under this Act shall be set off against the amount payable under such decree and the decree shall, notwithstanding anything contained in the Code of Civil Procedure, 1908 (5 of 1908), or any other law for the time being in force, be executable for the balance amount, if any, left after such set off.

(3) Every application under sub-section (1) shall be in such form and contain such particulars as may be prescribed or as nearly as possible thereto.

(4) The Magistrate shall fix the first date of hearing, which shall not ordinarily be beyond three days from the date of receipt of the application by the court.

(5) The Magistrate shall endeavour to dispose of every application made under sub-section (1) within a period of sixty days from the date of its first hearing.

Section 17 (Chapter 17) : Service of Notice

13. *Service of notice.*—(1) A notice of the date of hearing fixed under section 12 shall be given by the Magistrate to the Protection Officer, who shall get it served by such means as may be prescribed on the respondent, and on any other person, as directed by the Magistrate within a maximum period of two days or such further reasonable time as may be allowed by the Magistrate from the date of its receipt.

(2) A declaration of service of notice made by the Protection Officer in such form as may be prescribed shall be the proof that such notice was served upon the respondent and on any other person as directed by the Magistrate unless the contrary is proved.

Section 18 (Chapter 18) : Counselling

14. *Counselling.*—(1) The Magistrate may, at any stage of the proceedings under this Act, direct the respondent or the aggrieved person, either singly or jointly, to undergo counselling with any member of a service provider who possess such qualifications and experience in counselling as may be prescribed.

(2) Where the Magistrate has issued any direction under sub-section (1), he shall fix the next date of hearing of the case within a period not exceeding two months.

Section 19 (Chapter 19) : Assistance of Welfare Expert

15. *Assistance of welfare expert.*—In any proceeding under this Act, the Magistrate may secure the services of such person, preferably a woman, whether related to the aggrieved person or not, including a person engaged in promoting family welfare as he thinks fit, for the purpose of assisting him in discharging his functions.

Section 20 (Chapter 20) : Proceedings to be held in Camera

16. *Proceedings to be held in camera*.-If the Magistrate considers that the circumstances of the case so warrant, and if either party to the proceedings so desires, he may conduct the proceedings under this Act in camera.

Section 21 (Chapter 21) : Right to Reside in a Shared Household

17. *Right to reside in a shared household.*—(1) Notwithstanding anything contained in any other law for the time being in force, every woman in a domestic relationship shall have the right to reside in the shared household, whether or not she has any right, title or beneficial interest in the same.

(2) The aggrieved person shall not be evicted or excluded from the shared household or any part of it by the respondent save in accordance with the procedure established by law.

Section 22 (Chapter 22) : Protection Orders:

18. *Protection orders.*—The Magistrate may, after giving the aggrieved person and the respondent an opportunity of being heard and on being *prima facie* satisfied that domestic iolence has taken place or is likely to take place, pass a protection order in favour of the aggrieved person and prohibit the respondent from—

(a) committing any act of domestic violence;
(b) aiding or abetting in the commission of acts of domestic violence;
(c) entering the place of employment of the aggrieved person or, if the person aggrieved is a child, its school or any other place frequented by the aggrieved person;
(d) attempting to communicate in any form, whatsoever, with the aggrieved person, including personal, oral or written or electronic or telephonic contact;
(e) alienating any assets, operating bank lockers or bank accounts used or held or enjoyed by both the parties, jointly by the aggrieved person and the respondent or singly by the respondent, including her stridhan or any other property held either jointly by the parties or

separately by them without the leave of the Magistrate;

(f) causing violence to the dependants, other relatives or any person who give the aggrieved person assistance from domestic violence; and

(g) committing any other act as specified in the protection order.

Section 23 (Chapter 23) Residence Orders

19. *Residence orders*.—(1) While disposing of an application under sub-section (1) of section 12, the Magistrate may, on being satisfied that domestic violence has taken place, pass a residence order :

(a) restraining the respondent from dispossessing or in any other manner disturbing the possession of the aggrieved person from the shared household, whether or not the respondent has a legal or equitable interest in the shared household;

(b) directing the respondent to remove himself from the shared household;

(c) restraining the respondent or any of his relatives from entering any portion of the shared household in which the aggrieved person resides;

(d) restraining the respondent from alienating or disposing-off the shared household or encumbering the same;

(e) restraining the respondent from renouncing his rights in the shared household except with the leave of the Magistrate; or

(f) directing the respondent to secure same level of alternate accommodation for the aggrieved person as enjoyed by her in the shared household or to pay rent for the same, if the circumstances so require: Provided that no order under clause (b) shall be passed against any person who is a woman.

(2) The Magistrate may impose any additional conditions or pass any other direction which he may deem reasonably necessary to protect or to provide for the safety of the aggrieved person or any child of such aggrieved person.

(3) The Magistrate may require from the respondent to execute a bond, with or without sureties, for preventing the commission of domestic violence.

(4) An order under sub-section (3) shall be deemed to be an order under Chapter VIII of the Code of Criminal Procedure, 1973 (2 of 1974) and shall be dealt with accordingly.

(5) While passing an order under sub-section (1), sub-section (2) or sub-section (3), the court may also pass an order directing the officer in charge of the nearest police station to give protection to the aggrieved person or to assist her or the person making an application on her behalf in the implementation of the order.

(6) While making an order under sub-section (1), the Magistrate may impose on the respondent obligations relating to the discharge of rent and other payments, having regard to the financial needs and resources of the parties.

(7) The Magistrate may direct the officer in-charge of the police station in whose jurisdiction the Magistrate has been approached to assist in the implementation of the protection order.

(8) The Magistrate may direct the respondent to return to the possession of the aggrieved person her stridhan or any other property or valuable security to which she is entitled to.

Section 24 (Chapter 24) : Monetary relief

20. *Monetary relief.*—(1) While disposing of an application under sub-section (1) of section 12, the Magistrate may direct the respondent to pay monetary relief to meet the expenses incurred and losses suffered by the aggrieved person and any child of the aggrieved person as a result of the domestic violence and such relief may include, but not limited to,—

(a) the loss of earnings;
(b) the medical expenses;
(c) the loss caused due to the destruction, damage or removal of any property from the control of the aggrieved person; and
(d) the maintenance for the aggrieved person as well as her children, if any, including an order under or in

addition to an order of maintenance under section 125 of the Code of Criminal Procedure, 1973 (2 of 1974) or any other law for the time being in force.

(2) The monetary relief granted under this section shall be adequate, fair and reasonable and consistent with the standard of living to which the aggrieved person is accustomed.

(3) The Magistrate shall have the power to order an appropriate lump sum payment or monthly payments of maintenance, as the nature and circumstances of the case may require.

(4) The Magistrate shall send a copy of the order for monetary relief made under sub-section (1) to the parties to the application and to the in charge of the police station within the local limits of whose jurisdiction the respondent resides.

(5) The respondent shall pay the monetary relief granted to the aggrieved person within the period specified in the order under sub-section (1).

(6) Upon the failure on the part of the respondent to make payment in terms of the order under sub-section (1), the Magistrate may direct the employer or a debtor of the respondent, to directly pay to the aggrieved person or to deposit with the court a portion of the wages or salaries or debt due to or accrued to the credit of the respondent, which amount may be adjusted towards the monetary relief payable by the respondent.

Section 25 (Chapter 25) : Custody Orders

21. Custody orders.-Notwithstanding anything contained in any other law for the time being in force, the Magistrate may, at any stage of hearing of the application for protection order or for any other relief under this Act grant temporary custody of any child or children to the aggrieved person or the person making an application on her behalf and specify, if necessary, the arrangements for visit of such child or children by the respondent:Provided that if the Magistrate is of the opinion that any visit of the respondent may be harmful to the interests of the child or children, the Magistrate shall refuse to allow such visit.

Section 26 (Chapter 26) : Compensation Orders

22. Compensation orders.-In addition to other reliefs as may be granted under this Act, the Magistrate may on an application being made by the aggrieved person, pass an order directing the respondent to pay compensation and damages for the injuries, including mental torture and emotional distress, caused by the acts of domestic violence committed by that respondent.

Section 27 (Chapter 27) : Power to grant interim and exparte orders.

23. Power to grant interim and ex parte orders.—(1) In any proceeding before him under this Act, the Magistrate may pass such interim order as he deems just and proper.

(2) If the Magistrate is satisfied that an application *prima facie* discloses that the respondent is committing, or has committed an act of domestic violence or that there is a likelihood that the respondent may commit an act of domestic violence, he may grant an *ex parte* order on the basis of the affidavit in such form, as may be prescribed, of the aggrieved person under section 18, section 19, section 20, section 21 or, as the case may be, section 22 against the respondent..

Section 28 (Chapter 28) : Court to give Copies of Order Free of Cost

24. *Court to give copies of order free of cost.*—The Magistrate shall, in all cases where he has passed any order under this Act, order that a copy of such order, shall be given free of cost, to the parties to the application, the police officer in-charge of the police station in the jurisdiction of which the Magistrate has been approached, and any service provider located within the local limits of the jurisdiction of the court and if any service provider has registered a domestic incident report, to that service provider.

Section 29 (Chapter 29) : Duration and Alteration of orders

25. *Duration and alteration of orders.*—(1) A protection order made under section 18 shall be in force till the aggrieved person applies for discharge.

(2) If the Magistrate, on receipt of an application from the aggrieved person or the respondent, is satisfied that there is a change in the circumstances requiring alteration, modification or revocation of any order made under this Act, he may, for reasons to be recorded in writing pass such order, as he may deem appropriate.

Section 30 (Chapter 30) : Relief in Other Suits and Legal Proceedings

26. *Relief in other suits and legal proceedings.*—(1) Any relief available under sections 18, 19, 20, 21 and 22 may also be sought in any legal proceeding, before a civil court, family court or a criminal court, affecting the aggrieved person and the respondent whether such proceeding was initiated before or after the commencement of this Act.

(2) Any relief referred to in sub-section (1) may be sought for in addition to and along with any other relief that the aggrieved person may seek in such suit or legal proceeding before a civil or criminal court.

(3) In case any relief has been obtained by the aggrieved person in any proceedings other than a proceeding under this Act, she shall be bound to inform the Magistrate of the grant of such relief.

Section 31 (Chapter 31) : Jurisdiction

27. *Jurisdiction.*—(1) The court of Judicial Magistrate of the first class or the Metropolitan Magistrate, as the case may be, within the local limits of which—

(a) the person aggrieved permanently or temporarily resides or carries on business or is employed; or

(b) the respondent resides or carries on business or is employed; or

(c) the cause of action has arisen, shall be the competent court to grant a protection order and other orders under this Act and to try offences under this Act.

(2) Any order made under this Act shall be enforceable throughout India.

Section 32 (Chapter 32) : Procedures

28. *Procedure.*—(1) Save as otherwise provided in this Act, all proceedings under sections 12, 18, 19, 20, 21, 22 and 23 and offences under section 31 shall be governed by the provisions of the Code of Criminal Procedure, 1973 (2 of 1974).

(2) Nothing in sub-section (1) shall prevent the court from laying down its own procedure for disposal of an application under section 12 or under sub-section (2) of section 23.

Section 33 (Chapter 33) : Appeal

29. *Appeal.*—There shall lie an appeal to the Court of Session within thirty days from the date on which the order made by the Magistrate is served on the aggrieved person or the respondent, as the case may be, whichever is later.

Section 35 (Chapter 35) : Protection Officers and Members of Service Providers to be Public Servants

30. *Protection Officers and members of service providers to be public servants.*—The Protection Officers and members of service providers, while acting or purporting to act in pursuance of any of the provisions of this Act or any rules or orders made thereunder shall be deemed to be public servants within the meaning of section 21 of the Indian Penal Code (45 of 1860).

Section 36 (Chapter 36) : Penalty for Breach of Protection Order by Respondent

31. *Penalty for breach of protection order by respondent.*—(1) A breach of protection order, or of an interim protection order, by the respondent shall be an offence under this Act and shall be punishable with imprisonment of either description for a term which may extend to one year, or with fine which may extend to twenty thousand rupees, or with both.

(2) The offence under sub-section (1) shall as far as practicable be tried by the Magistrate who had passed the order, the breach of which has been alleged to have been caused by the accused.

(3) While framing charges under sub-section (1), the Magistrate may also frame charges under *section 498A* of the

Indian Penal Code (45 of 1860) or any other provision of that Code or the *Dowry Prohibition Act*, 1961 (28 of 1961), as the case may be, if the facts disclose the commission of an offence under those provisions.

Section 37 (Chapter 37) : Cognizance and Proof

32. *Cognizance and proof.*—(1) Notwithstanding anything contained in the Code of Criminal Procedure, 1973 (2 of 1974), the offence under sub-section (1) of section 31 shall be cognizable and non-bailable.

(2) Upon the sole testimony of the aggrieved person, the court may conclude that an offence under sub-section (1) of section 31 has been committed by the accused.

Section 38 (Chapter 38) : Penalty for not Discharging Duty by Protection Officer

33. *Penalty for not discharging duty by Protection Officer.*—If any Protection Officer fails or refuses to discharge his duties as directed by the Magistrate in the protection order without any sufficient cause, he shall be punished with imprisonment of either description for a term which may extend to one year, or with fine which may extend to twenty thousand rupees, or with both.

Section 39 (Chapter 39) : Cognizance of Offence Committed by Protection Officer

34. *Cognizance of offence committed by Protection Officer.*—No prosecution or other legal proceeding shall lie against the Protection Officer unless a complaint is filed with the previous sanction of the State Government or an officer authorised by it in this behalf.

Section 40 (Chapter 40) : Protection of Action taken in Good Faith

35. *Protection of action taken in good faith.*—No suit, prosecution or other legal proceeding shall lie against the Protection Officer for any damage caused or likely to be caused by anything which is in good faith done or intended to be done under this Act or any rule or order made thereunder.

Section 41 (Chapter 41) : Act not in Derogation of any Other Law

36. *Act not in derogation of any other law.*—The provisions of this Act shall be in addition to, and not in derogation of the provisions of any other law, for the time being in force.

Section 42 (Chapter 42) : Power of Central Government to make Rules

37. *Power of Central Government to make rules.*—(1) The Central Government may, by notification, make rules for carrying out the provisions of this Act.

(2) In particular, and without prejudice to the generality of the foregoing power, such rules may provide for all or any of the following matters, namely:

(a) the qualifications and experience which a Protection Officer shall possess under sub-section (2) of section 8;
(b) the terms and conditions of service of the Protection Officers and the other officers subordinate to him, under sub-section (3) of section 8;
(c) the form and manner in which a domestic incident report may be made under clause (b) of sub-section (1) of section 9;
(d) the form and the manner in which an application for protection order may be made to the Magistrate under clause (c) of sub-section (1) of section 9;
(e) the form in which a complaint is to be filed under clause (d) of sub-section (1) of section 9;
(f) the other duties to be performed by the Protection Officer under clause (i) of sub-section (1) of section 9;
(g) the rules regulating registration of service providers under sub-section (1) of section 10;
(h) the form in which an application under sub-section (1) of section 12 seeking reliefs under this Act may be made and the particulars which such application shall contain under sub-section (3) of that section;
(i) the means of serving notices under sub-section (1) of section 13;
(j) the form of declaration of service of notice to be made

by the Protection Officer under sub-section (2) of section 13;

(k) the qualifications and experience in counselling which a member of the service provider shall possess under sub-section (1) of section 14;

(l) the form in which an affidavit may be filed by the aggrieved person under sub-section (2) of section 23; and

(m) any other matter which has to be, or may be, prescribed.

(3) Every rule made under this Act shall be laid, as soon as may be after it is made, before each House of Parliament, while it is in session, for a total period of thirty days which may be comprised in one session or in two or more successive sessions, and if, before the expiry of the session immediately following the session or the successive sessions aforesaid, both Houses agree in making any modification in the rule or both Houses agree that the rule should not be made, the rule shall thereafter have effect only in such modified form or be of no effect, as the case may be; so, however, that any such modification or annulment shall be without prejudice to the validity of anything previously done under that rule.

SD/- BRAHM AVTAR AGRAWAL
Addl. Secretary to the Government of India

Notes and References

1. www.vakilno1.com/bareacts/Domestic-Violence/Domestic-Violence-Act-2005.htm
2. http://www.vakilno1.com/bareacts/IndianPenalCode/S498A.htm
3. http://www.vakilno1.com/bareacts/IndianPenalCode/indianpenalcode.htm

Bibliography

Alexander, Robert J., *The Entrepreneur, The Manager and Economic Development,* MacMillan Company, New York, 1962.

Altekar, A.S., The Position of Women in Hindu Civilisation, 1974, Verry Lawrence Inc. Connecticut.

Anderson, Robert Lee and Dunkelbert, John D., *Entrepreneurship,* Harper and Row Publishers, New York.

Anna, V., Socio-Economic Basis of Women Entrepreneurship, *SEDME,* Vol. 17, No. 1, 1990.

Anthony, M.J., Women Rights (1985), Dialogue Publication, New Delhi.

Austin, Granville, The Indian Constitution—The Cornerstone of a Nation (1966).

Azad, Gulab Singh, Development of Entrepreneurship Among Indian Women, *SEDME,* Vol. XVI, No. 3, 1989.

Azad, Maulana, Abul Kalam, Tarjuman-ul-Quran, Sahitya Academic, New Delhi.

Baminidi, Devi Prasad: Gender and Dowry Related Violence against Women: Some Case Studies, *I.J. of Criminology and Criminalistics,* Vol. 10, Jan.-Dec. 1990, pp. 33-48.

Banerji, A., Sen, R.K., Women and Economic Development, Deep & Deep Publications Pvt. Ltd., New Delhi, 2003.

Baron, A.S., Women in Management, Another Look, *Personnel Administrator,* Vol. 29, August 1984, p. 14.

Bhatia, B.S. *et. al.,* Women Entrepreneurship: Explored and Unexplored Opportunities, *Gender Sensitivity,* TTTI, Chandigarh, 2000.

Bhatia, B.S., New Industrial Entrepreneurs: Their Origin and Problems, *Journal of General Management,* Vol. 2, No. I, Autumn 1975.

Bisht, Narendra S. and Sharma, Pamila K., *Entrepreneurship: Expectations and Experiences,* Himalaya Publishing House, New Delhi, 1991, Blackstone, Commentaries on the Laws of England (1925).

Callision, I.P.: A Layman Looks at Justice, *Journal of America Indicative Society,* 176, April 1963.

Cannon, T. *et. al., The Nature, the Role and the Impact of Small Business Research,* Glower, Alder Shot, 1989.

Carter, S. and Cannon, T., *Women as Entrepreneurs: A Study of Female Business Owners, Their Motivations, Experiences and Strategies for Success,* Academic Press, London, 1992.

Casson, Mark, *The Entrepreneur: An Economic Theory,* Martin Robertson, Oxford, 1982.

Chandra, Shanti Kohli, *Development of Women Entrepreneurship* in *India,* Mittal Publications, New Delhi, 1991, p. 70.

Chaudhary, P.K., Bhaiji, S. and Asokan, M., Banks and Women's Enterprise Development: A Comparison of Approaches in India and U.K., *SEDME,* 1997.

Chhina, S.S., Women Labour : Problem and Policy Implications, Regal Publications, New Delhi, 2009.

Daftary, Sharayu, Women and Business: An Untapped Potential, *Journal of the Indian Merchants Chamber,* 75(12), December 1981, pp. 9-10.

Dash, Anita, Women Industrial Workers, Regal Publications, New Delhi, 2009

Derett: Nullity of Marriage Among Hindus, AIR 1964, General Section, p. 957.

Desingu, Setty, E., Developing Entrepreneurship among Women, *Man and Development,* 2(3), September 1980, pp. 92-96.

Dhagamwar, Vasudhu, Woman and Divorce (1987), Somaiya Publication Pvt. Ltd., Bombay.

Dhameja, S.K., Women Entrepreneurs : Opportunities, Performance and Problems, Deep & Deep Publications Pvt. Ltd., New Delhi, 2008.

Dhar, Lalita: Dowry Litigation in India: Retrospects and Prospects, *Indian Social Legal Journal,* Vol. 14, 16, 1989-90, pp. 127-41.

Diwan, Paras, Dowry and Protection to Married Women (1995), Deep and Deep Publications, New Delhi.

Dolinsky, Arthur L., Caputo, Richard K. and Pasumarty, Kishore, Long-term Entrepreneurship Patterns: A National Study of Black and White Female Entry and Stayer Status Differences, *Journal of Small Business Management,* January, Vol. 32, 1994.

Ewener, J.A., Portrait of Two Artists as Young Entrepreneurs, *Canadian Business,* Vol. 58, September 1985, p. 166.

Finney, S. Ruth, *Towards a Typology of Women Entrepreneurs—Their Business Venture and Family,* East-West Centre, East-West Technology and Development Institute, Honololu, Hawaii (USA), 1977.

Flerida Ruth P. Romero, Women and Law, U.P. Law Centre, The Asia Foundation (1983).

Freidmann, Law in a Changing Society (1950), University Broth. House, Delhi.

Gandhi, Indira, Self-Employment for Women, *Social Welfare,* 28(10), January 1982, pp. 1-2.

Ghosh, S.K., Women and Crime, Ashish Publishing House, New Delhi.

Goel, A., Kaur, M., Sultana, A., Violence against Women : Issues and Perspectives, Deep & Deep Publications Pvt. Ltd., New Delhi, 2006.

Goel, Aruna, Women Empowerment : Myth or Reality, Deep & Deep Publications Pvt. Ltd., New Delhi, 2009.

Gokilavani, S., Suba, S., Communal Riots and Women Victims, Regal Publications, New Delhi, 2009.

Gokilavani, S., Jelestin, S.G., Regal Publications, New Delhi, 2008.

Hamilton, Hedayas, 1945, Harbison, F. and Myers, Charles A., *Education, Manpower and Economic Growth: Strategies of Human Resources Development,* New York, McGraw Hill Service in International Development.

Hemlata, D., Attitude to Dowry System, *Social Welfare,* Vol. 30, pp. 13-14.

Hisrich, Robert D. and Fuldop, Gyula, Women Entrepreneurs in Controlled Economies: A Hungarian Perspective, *Frontiers of Entrepreneurship Research,* Massachusetts (USA), 1993.

Islam Sirajul, Directive Principles of State Policy in Indian Constitution, 75 (1988) 2 SCC 503.

John, Usha, Emerging Corporate Women, *Economic Times* (Supplement), 25 November 1981, pp. 11:1-5.

Kanitkar, Ajit and Contractor, Nalinee; *In Search of Identity—The Women Entrepreneurs of India,* EDI(I), Ahmedabad, 1992.

Khan, M.T. and Roy, R., Dowry Death, *Indian Journal of Social Work,* Vol. 55, 1984, pp. 303-15.

Kilby, Peter (Ed.), *Entrepreneurship and Economic Development,* The Free Press, New York, 1971.

Kirve, Harsha and Kanitkar, Ajit, Entrepreneurship at the Grass-roots: Developing the Income Generating Capabilities of Rural Women, *The Journal of Entrepreneurship,* Volume 2, No. 2, 1993.

Krishan Mahajan: Fixing Women's Legal Future: Misconception on Women's Law (National Seminar on Women and the Law), 17th and 18th October 1981.

Kumar, A., Women Entrepreneurship in India, Regal Publications, New Delhi, 2007

Kumar, B., Globalisation and Women Empowerment : Multidimensional Approaches, Deep & Deep Publications Pvt. Ltd., New Delhi, 2009.

Kumar, B., Women Empowerment and Sustainable Development, Regal Publications, New Delhi, 2009.

Lasser, J.K., *How to Run a Small Business,* McGraw Hill Book Co., New York, 1963.

Layman, A., Women in Family Business: An Untapped Resource, *Advance Management Journal,* Vol. 50, Winter.

Martin, J. and Roberts, C., *Women and Employment: A Life Time Perspective,* Report of the 1980 DE/OPCS Women and Employment Survey, HMSO, London, 1984

Mathey, Attitude Towards Dowry, *Indian Journal of Social Work,* Vol. 48, 1987, pp. 93-101.

McClelland, D.C., *et. al., Motivating Economic Achievement,* The Free Press, New York, 1969.

Mujamdar, Vina, Women in the Developing Economy, *General Editors,* Vols. I and II.

Nageswari, R., Gokilavani, S., Women's Consumer Rights and their Awareness, Regal Publications, New Delhi, 2007.

Naik, R.D., A Study of Dowry Practise in Greater Bombay, *Social Defence*, Vol. 25-26 (1988), pp. 37-46.

Nair, M. Krishan, Public Interest Litigation, *Cochin University Law Review*, pp. 489-90.

Nayak, Nalini, A Struggle within the Struggle, 1986, Programme for Community Organisation, Spener Junction, Trivandrum.

Olson, Shirley F. and Currie, Helen, M., Female Entrepreneurs: Personal Value Systems and Business Strategies in a Male-Dominated Industry, *Journal of Small Business Management*, January 1992.

Paise, See Suzanne Panandiker, Surekha, Management of Enterprise, *The Economic Times*, Delhi, 26 Dec. 1985.

Pal, B.K., Problems and Concern of Indian Women, 1987, ABC Publishing House.

Paul, M.C., Dowry and Position of Women in India, Inter-India Pub., New Delhi, p. 16, pp. 66-98.

Price, Courtney and Monroe, Stuart, Educational Training for Women and Minority Entrepreneurs Positively Impacts Venture Growth and Development, *Frontiers of Entrepreneurship Research*, Massachusetts, USA, 1993.

Rajula Davi, A.K., Women Entrepreneurs, *Yojana*, 22(13), 16 July 1978, pp. 19-22.

Raju, M.L., Women Empowerment : Challenges and Strategies, Regal Publications, New Delhi, 2007.

Rao, V.V. and Rao, N., Marriage, The Family and Women in India, Heritage Publishers, New Delhi (1982).

Rathore, B.S. and Dhameja, S.K. (Eds.), *Entrepreneurship in the 21st Century*, Rawat Publications, Jaipur, 1999.

Sahasranaman, Meenakshi, Special Problems of Women Entrepreneurs, *Women's Era* (India), 2 April 1978, pp. 17-21.

Saini, J.S., Dhameja, S.K. and Gupta, S.K., *Case Studies of TITI Trained Entrepreneurs*, TITI, Chandigarh Publication, 1990.

Saini, J.S. and Dhameja, S.K. (Eds.), *Entrepreneurship and Small Business*, Rawat Publications, Jaipur, 1998.

———, *Entrepreneurship Development*, Deep and Deep Publications, New Delhi, 1996.

Saxena, Shobha, Crimes against Women and Protective Laws, Deep & Deep Publications Pvt. Ltd., New Delhi, 2008.

Sharma, D.D., Dhameja, S.K. and Gurjar, B.R. (Eds.), *Entrepreneurship, Strategic Management and Globalisation*, Rawat Publications, Jaipur, 1998.

Sharma, Rashmi, Women Development : New Approaches and Innovation, Regal Publications, New Delhi, 2009.

Sharma, Rashmi, Women, Law and Judicial System, Regal Publications, New Delhi, 2009.

Sharma, Vinay, Dowry Deaths : Legal Provisions and Judicial Interpretation, Deep & Deep Publications Pvt. Ltd., New Delhi, 2007.

Siddiqui, Saif , Women Entrepreneurs in Export Trade, Regal Publications, New Delhi, 2008.

Sinha, A.K., New Dimensions of Women Empowerment, Deep & Deep Publications Pvt. Ltd., New Delhi, 2008.

———, Rural Women Workforce, Regal Publiations, New Delhi, 2009.

Stevenson, L., *'An Investigation of the Entrepreneurial Experience of Women: Implications for Small Business Policy* in *Canada'*, Acadia University, Wofville, Nova Scotia, November 1983.

Thakur, A.K., Rahman, R., Women Entrepreneurship, Deep & Deep Publications Pvt. Ltd., New Delhi, 2009.

Tinani, Madan, *Trainer's Manual on Entrepreneurship Development*, Singapore, Technonet Asia, 1981, p. 7.

Uprit *et al:* Parental Activity and Attitude of Women Students Towards Marriage and Dowry, *Social Welfare*, Vol. 45, No. 3, pp. 245-53.

Verghese, Jamila, Her Gold and Her Body, Vikas Publishing House Pvt. Ltd., (1980).

Verma, S.B., Status of Women in Modern India, Deep & Deep Publications Pvt. Ltd., New Delhi, 2005.

Vinze, Medha Dubashi, *Women Entrepreneurs* in *India: A Socio-Economic Study of Delhi*, 1975-85, Mittal Publications, Delhi, 1987.

White, J., The Rise of Female Capitalism: Women as Entrepreneurs, *Business Quarterly*, Vol. 49, September 1984, pp. 133-35.

Winston, Sandra, *The Entrepreneurial Women*, Newsweek Books, New York, 1979.

Zinkin, Maurice, "Entrepreneurs: Key to Growth," *Stanford Research Institute Journal*, Second Quarter, 1961.

Index